"In this seminal work, Greenwell provides us with a detailed understanding of how to respond to both the sublime and beatific realizations, and the emotional and mental challenges that naturally arise as one integrates transcendent wisdom with everyday life. *When Spirit Leaps* is a must-read for all who wish to understand the complexities and pitfalls that occur, in one form or another, to all who are engaged in the process of spiritual awakening."

— **Richard Miller, PhD**, past president of the Institute for Spirituality and Psychology, and author of *The iRest Program for Healing PTSD* and *Yoga Nidra*

"Bonnie Greenwell is a wonderful guide for both the awakening of mind and of your body's energies. Understanding energy work is an important bridge between the two worlds of infinite awareness and everyday reality, which has not been clearly described, and yet is so important for the unfolding awakening. You will find *When Spirit Leaps* a gift in navigating the awakening process of body, mind, and spirit."

— **Loch Kelly**, author *Shift into Freedom*

"Some spiritual seekers mistake intellectual understanding for Realization. Others have a genuine Awakening, but are frightened or confused by the experience because they don't understand it. I think that seekers should consider the cultivation of both experience and understanding a lifelong project, as Bonnie has done. One of the fruits of her dedication, which is rare among spiritual teachers and writers, is that she appreciates the multidimensional nature of reality, and is thus comfortable embracing paradox. I think you will find this one of the more useful and memorable spiritual books you have ever read."

— **Rick Archer**, *Buddha at the Gas Pump*

"Any time a great writer tries to tackle higher consciousness, they can get lost in their own dogma. Bonnie Greenwell's new book does not get lost—it represents a lifetime commitment to help raise humanity's awareness of higher consciousness, how to live with an awakened kundalini, and offers wonderful, simple exercises that can help the process along the path in a clear and positive manner. Bonnie has put forth her lifetime of working with and studying people in the process of self-realization and even God realization. The end of the book shows insights into what this really means: that perfection is never 100 percent perfection, and awareness of this is awareness of what it really is in and of itself. It is a masterpiece of divine words with a pure heart and positive message. Anyone who reads this book will benefit from the experience."

—**Tom Kay**, founder of www.ecomall.com, www.cybergod.com, and the last person to interview Gopi Krishna

"*When Spirit Leaps* is the essential guide for spiritual awakening and transformation. It is for both the awakened teacher and the truth seeker in transition. It is also essential for those of us who may know our path very well, but are not familiar with other paths. One size does not fit all, and it is very important not to be dogmatic in our approach. This guide helps teachers see there are more ways than one. It is a profound, loving, and thorough book. In Zen it is said, 'If you want to know the way up the mountain, ask someone who comes and goes on it.' Bonnie Greenwell is such a one."

—**Tom Thompson**, spiritual teacher and consultant for over forty years; cofounder and director of The Awakened Heart Center for Conscious Living in Pittsboro, NC

"Bonnie Greenwell's new book *When Spirit Leaps* summarizes in a pragmatic fashion over thirty years of her psychospiritual practice, research, and personal experience about how to make one's way through the process of spiritual awakening in a lucid, inspiring way. Regardless of whether one's awakening experiences were spontaneous or the result of years of yoga or meditation practice, or whether they have been blissful, crisis-filled, or something in-between, this book takes you through many key components of how spirit can unfold within our awareness, including the areas of kundalini and non-duality. It will be of great benefit to experiencers, spiritual teachers, or health professionals that specialize in this emerging field."

—**Ted Esser, PhD**, spiritual counselor, former director of
the Spiritual Emergence Network, and assistant chair for
the psychology department at Sofia University

"This is a deeply touching, transforming, and empowering book. Different from inspirational autobiographical accounts of those seekers who suddenly found themselves in touch with spiritual realities of their minds, this book is written by an experienced psychologist, researcher, and trained clinician. Bonnie Greenwell used her professional skills in service to the spiritual search. As a result, the book both inspires and provides practical, pragmatic tools to one's own process of spiritual awakening and transformation. Most importantly, the book overcomes an illusory division between the spirit and the body by grounding spiritual awakening in lived reality of one's embodied every day.... Like Bonnie's earlier books, this volume is destined to become an instant spiritual classic."

—**Olga Louchakova-Schwartz, MD, PhD**, professor emerita of
psychology and comparative religion at the former (1975-2014)
Institute of Transpersonal Psychology

WHEN SPIRIT LEAPS

Navigating the Process of
Spiritual Awakening

BONNIE L. GREENWELL, PhD

NON-DUALITY PRESS
An Imprint of New Harbinger Publications

Publisher's Note

Distributed in Canada by Raincoast Books

Copyright © 2018 by Bonnie L. Greenwell
        Non-Duality Press
        An imprint of New Harbinger Publications, Inc.
        5674 Shattuck Avenue
        Oakland, CA 94609
        www.newharbinger.com

Cover design by Amy Shoup

Acquired by Catharine Meyers

Edited by Jennifer Holder

All Rights Reserved

Library of Congress Cataloging-in-Publication Data on file

20   19   18

10   9   8   7   6   5   4   3   2   1   First Printing

CONTENTS

FOREWORD
BY ADYASHANTI

There are moments when the habitual veils of consensus reality part and the heart quickens as new, unexpected vistas of experience and perception unfold within you, gifting your mind and body with what our ancestors called revelation. Like the spirit of God descending upon Jesus in the river Jordan, or the Buddha awakening under the bodhi tree after years of ascetic deprivation, there are moments when you are suddenly gifted with the fire of spiritual realization. These moments may be brief and fleeting or they may be deeply transformative, even disorienting, but either way once you are kissed with your own true nature you will have embarked upon a road less traveled, where new vistas of perception and experience unfold that will both amaze and challenge you to embody your true nature within body, mind, and spirit.

When Spirit Leaps is more than a clever title for this wonderful book. It signifies an already present reality as well as a living potential within us all. It speaks of awakening from the constrictive dream of the imagined self to our true nature, and the embodiment of that realization in our daily life. This leap is not a leap of faith, nor a change of belief system, still less a form of unending self-improvement. This leap is a leap of the spirit, of our true nature awakening into conscious recognition of itself. It is a leap out of the consensus dream of separation to the awakened view of life as it actually is: complete, whole, and all inclusive. Such awakening renders the world of time transparent to the transcendent light of eternity, and it opens a door to a whole new world of possibilities where eternal truth is not just experienced, but lived and embodied in the relative world.

I have known the author of this fine book, Bonnie Greenwell, for many years. First as a student, then as someone who I asked to teach many years ago, and now as a beloved friend. Bonnie draws upon a lifetime of dedication to spirituality, psychology, and the study of kundalini energy. *When Spirit Leaps* is a book full of practical and powerful spiritual teachings, *dharma*, that delve into the minutia of spiritual experience in a way that is rarely done. It is an expression of Bonnie's great love and dedication to the dharma and to helping all who feel the yearning toward freedom, or God, to awaken to their true nature.

Contrary to the idea that a moment of awakening is the end of spiritual development, *When Spirit Leaps* is a book that also speaks to the deeper waters of spiritual realization beyond the experience of awakening. And it is here that Bonnie's vast experience comes into full view. Her knowledge of psychology provides a welcome and balanced perspective of the spiritual path, as does her intimate knowledge of the role that kundalini energy plays in the unfolding of our spiritual evolution.

The world today is in great need of higher consciousness, deeper wisdom, and more expansive love. If we are to meet the great challenges that humanity faces, each one of us must step forward and take responsibility for the evolution of our consciousness, for no one can do it for us and the consequences of failing to do so become greater day by day. Fortunately we all possess the potential for greater love and wisdom than we can imagine. And it is for this purpose that *When Spirit Leaps* was written. It is a testament to our true nature, which is always and already fully present if we simply stop to recognize what we have always been just beneath the veil of our imagination.

So read this book as good medicine and sacred guidance. Take it to heart and put it into practice, and you will begin to see and experience your true nature coming into conscious recognition of itself as the doors of your unfathomable potential begin to open.

INTRODUCTION

I was hiking on an island and looked out across the water to nearby land. Suddenly I saw that everything inside me was outside me, and everything outside was inside. There was no separation. The water, hills, trees, earth were in me—and my bones, blood, flesh, organs were in them. We were all one. Later, back in the group retreat, there was a sensation of everyone being boundaryless. These experiences created a deep sense of awe, full of spacious awareness.

Louise told me this story, one of thousands I have gathered from more than thirty years of counseling people who have had flashes of awakening. It is a moment when spirit leapt. I titled this book *When Spirit Leaps* to capture the essence of sudden awakening. I was inspired by an ancient Zen tradition described by Adyashanti, who spent fifteen years doing Zen practices. He said that, in earlier times, a monitor would wander meditation halls holding a narrow stick, watching for anyone on the verge of spiritual awakening. When someone was close, he whacked the meditator on a shoulder blade with the stick, near the side of the neck. This jolted the meditator's energy upward through the head, and plunged him or her into *satori*—a sudden enlightenment. While this practice is no longer followed, spirit may still leap spontaneously in a meditative setting. It can even happen without any clear context during an activity as ordinary as a hike.

When spirit leaps, we can be jolted into an energized state, open to a sense of spaciousness, or feel free from our personal identity. We may find it blissful, radiant, joyful, or gently revelatory. This is grace. But this leap of the spirit can also feel challenging—particularly if there is no preparation, we have a traumatic event in our past, a history of addiction, or repressed memories of abuse. And if no one else understands the experience, the beauty and potential of an awakening may be discounted or suppressed.

An *awakening* is a major shift in consciousness that brings a radically different understanding of who we are. It is part of a spiritual journey to peace and wholeness, and often introduces an internal source of wisdom and alters the external expressions of our life. By pursuing this journey, we learn to feel at home in who we are, which—it turns out—is not who we thought we were. Awakening events along the way answer our longing for truth or God or oneness or realization. As the perception gained through awakening stabilizes, we no longer feel a need for spiritual searching.

Awakening occurs across cultures and is a universal human potential. Even though ample evidence for this exists, few spiritual teachers, meditation instructors, medical professionals, therapists, or yoga teachers know how to recognize the ways that awakening impacts us. Most are unable to offer support. *When Spirit Leaps* offers a useful paradigm for spiritual seekers and teachers alike, as it describes commonly experienced dynamics that happen as an awakening glimpse moves toward liberation. My goal is to help you understand these phenomena, feel supported as you encounter them, and gain tools that will help you trust the journey so you can allow yourself to relax as the process evolves.

I became interested in this work after my own awakening. I was fourteen when my mother suddenly died and my heart armored itself to protect me from love. My faith in God was shattered. As a young mother in the 1960s, I became involved in the encounter movement, which introduced me to my inner world. I realized how profoundly empty I felt and how this limited my life, so I began an eclectic search for meaning. During the next fifteen years, I began Jungian analysis, followed meditation practices in both yoga and Buddhist traditions, earned an MA in counseling psychology, then entered a doctoral program in transpersonal psychology that blended psychology, spiritual practice, and therapeutic bodywork.

One day, following a powerful breathwork session, energy poured through my body and brought an ecstasy I had never known before. It pulled me deeper and deeper into meditation practice. This awakening triggered a transformative process that was to impact every aspect of my personal and professional life. The energy has stayed vibrant and opened my life to many adventures. I wrote a dissertation on *kundalini* (as I'll soon discuss, this is the energy of awakening in yoga traditions), traveled to India, cofounded an organization related to kundalini research, began working internationally, and met my teacher Adyashanti—who opened me to a deeper level of knowing who I am.

Since 1990, I have been consulting and counseling men and women who are awakening within nearly every tradition, and many who awaken outside of traditions. My own journey and the experiences shared by thousands of clients have given me an appreciation of the many paths to realization and of awakening as a natural process. By sharing stories about this transformative journey in this book, I hope to convey awakening as a birthright for all who long for it. While the stories are real, the names have been changed.

To help people live with transformative experiences, I offer support that is drawn from my own experiments, years of listening to others, and research into the history of awakening in several cultures. It is based on a blend of dualistic and non-dual traditions, as I have been deeply impacted by both perspectives. I've learned to value the human experience as well as the capacity of consciousness to evolve and transcend our limitations. Adyashanti describes this well: "Spiritually, the human condition is a natural part of the evolution of consciousness trying to become conscious through a form… When a person wakes up, consciousness is evolving through a human form, until it moves beyond separation, and this is liberation."[1]

Among the many camps of spirituality, it is unusual for a non-dual teacher to appreciate *kundalini*, the yogic word for coiled energy in our spine that can be awakened on the spiritual journey. Often, non-dual teachers neither acknowledge nor address the many experiences that arise when this life-force energy is highly activated. Non-dual schools of thought often see human life as only an illusion, and are fond of saying that nothing exists, which extends to mind-body experiences. Students are encouraged to ignore phenomena.

On the other hand, those who believe kundalini is the mechanism that leads to enlightenment are often skeptical about the non-dual teaching that awakening can be sudden and without preparation. Their perspective is that the body is involved in transformation, which makes cultivation through practices essential.

I have a long history of standing in several camps simultaneously. Although I embrace knowing that nothing is happening from a non-dual perspective, I cannot avoid seeing the so-called dream-world of life with all its challenge, suffering, joy, and possibility. I feel we know and live in two worlds: infinite consciousness and ordinary expressions of material life. To me, we are the wondrous expressions of form within a timeless, unlimited vastness. We appear in order to have our experiences. In this book, I bring these views together. The opening story is an example of this approach because Louise experienced sudden awakening during a hike, and it occurred within the cultivating environment of a group retreat.

Another bridge I make in this book extends over the assumption that Christianity and Judaism are exclusively dualistic traditions. When we read and explore God—beyond the perspective of a churchgoer with a vested interest in the otherness of God and Jesus—to know him as the mystics knew him, we see that there are direct moments of union. Jesus can be heard offering non-dual teachings when he said, "I and my Father are one," "I am that I am," and "the kingdom of God is within you." The kabbalah is filled with images of union. This is why I include notions of the divine, mention God, and include mystical Judeo-Christian views in this book.

I hope you will find elements of your own story in these pages, which are meant to be absorbed on three levels: for your mind to understand and relax, for your spirit to resonate and trust what is happening to you, and for your own authentic activity in life to be inspired.

When Spirit Leaps describes the experiences of the awakening process that lead to liberation. It helps you recognize the many ways awakening is initiated and progresses in your life, supports both the joys and challenges of this journey, offers tools for transformation and grounding, and inspires expansions of consciousness within yourself and our world. It is my hope that you will explore these pages with an open mind and heart, be touched by the possibilities for awakening yourself and for supporting others, and feel the joy that engaging spiritual experience brings into my life and the lives of the people who share their stories with you.

PART ONE

HOW WE AWAKEN

1. Spiritual Experiences and the Gift of Awakening

There have likely been moments in your life when you asked big questions: "What is real?" "What is life all about?" "Is there a God?" For some of us, these questions arise in early childhood—especially when we feel we don't see the world as others do and don't seem to fit in. As adults, we may ask them after a crisis or in a moment when we realize that we are unfulfilled by relationships, work, or material accomplishments. We sense something important is still missing and long for completion. Moments like these frequently stir a search for more, for fresh answers to the puzzle of our existence. We feel called to understand what is actually true. We feel propelled into a spiritual search from within.

We can also be thrust into this journey without intending it. Even people who would never identify as spiritual sometimes find themselves awakening through activities that I've come to call "portals" to awakening. Here are some external things that can propel us to seek deeper truths.

A near-death experience (NDE)

Deep meditative practice

A traumatic event or injury

Yoga or qigong exercises

Suffering, despair, or grief

Encountering a guru or awakened teacher

Childbirth

An exercise found on the Internet

Experimentation with psychedelics

Devotional practice and prayer

A visitation, vision, or mystical dream

Breathing practices

A sudden *aha!* moment

A shamanic journey or treatment

Through these moments of expanded awareness, we recognize there is something much bigger than "me," that "I" is not limited to the boundary of personal consciousness. They instigate experience beyond our personal body-mind that is a powerful, and often life-changing, event. These are the ways a spiritual journey can begin.

Portals and initial experiences often inspire us to go deeper. Our glimpses open up more questions and we may seek more answers. Awakening may become a primary intention in our life, pulling us into an unfathomable longing, and laying the groundwork for enlightenment. Our yearning is an internal call for a transformative shift of consciousness.

What Is Awakening?

This transformational shift is called *awakening*. Spiritual awakening, from a non-dual perspective, is clearly remembering who you are: one with all existence. Therefore, the universal consciousness within you awakens itself. Some spiritual teachers say it is the remembrance or realization of our true nature, by our true nature. Awareness and consciousness are suddenly clear and expansive, undisturbed, and undivided by thought. The experience may be accompanied by great insight, ecstatic bliss, or a mystical infusion of light, love, and vision. Awakening can strike us like a bolt of energy or it may gently unravel through years of seeking truth. Joanne, a retired librarian, had an awakening while meditating at a retreat.

There was a sudden seeing of complete, white, brilliant stillness everywhere. There was no "me" thinking—there was nothing but white illumination and it was complete love. It was spacious, unbounded, undifferentiated, endless, and pure love. I became aware that everything is of love and there is nothing other than that. Also, within this brilliance arose little blobs of worry, angst, and thoughts. I immediately knew that every thought, worry, angst was only that—and nothing else. They just appeared and fell away, and were without substance in this complete and pure brilliance. There was only joy, awe, and amazement.

Joanne had a sudden thought about hanging on to the experience and making it last, and then felt a heavy curtain came down over the entire scene that brought the sensation of density in her body. Mental chatter arose and she came out of meditation. Her momentary awakening can be called a "glimpse of freedom" or a "touch of grace." Many who experience it feel distressed when it passes, but its transience can offer encouragement to keep entering the silence of meditation.

Awakening is an internal, evolutionary impulse that may draw us into new perceptions of human life and our true nature, forcing a radical realignment of how we live. Awakening is a sudden movement, or a series of shifts, that makes enlightenment possible.

What Is Enlightenment?

When awakening becomes stabilized, we may experience liberation—enlightenment. All of us have this potential because our true nature already exists within each of us. We become liberated from our old identifications, compulsions, demands, and suffering.

Enlightenment has been described in mystical literature from many traditions in expansive terms, such as a descent of divine grace or a dissolving of the personal self while merging with the cosmos. It has also been imagined, and exaggerated, as a permanently transcendent state of all-knowing wisdom and unending bliss, with miraculous powers. An ineffable spiritual experience is sometimes mistaken for enlightenment, but it is not. More often, enlightenment feels like opening into a quiet and subtle recognition of our true nature.

Enlightenment is the ability to live, day in and day out, in a state of union, free from conditioned separateness and division. It requires continual alignment with the truth we have seen while awakening. It is more enduring—and therefore more challenging—than having initial moments of awakening. Enlightenment requires plunging into the unknown mystery of transformation. Not many who have an initial awakening realization will continue the journey beyond to liberation, as most of us are content with the initial gift or become distracted with the demands and desires of life.

A common misperception about enlightenment is that it requires a kind of sainthood and purity that we know we will never possess. This ideal is based on stories of a few enlightened sages or saints. But these men and women are simply styles of enlightened living, because liberated lives vary as much as unawakened ones. Many great mystics, historical and modern, had lives in turmoil before they were liberated—and their enlightenment brought clarity rather than perfection. Enlightenment calls for authenticity, a willingness to listen to the deepest intuition about what right expression is from moment to moment. It brings an appreciation of the needs of the *whole* rather than caring only for the individual, limited *me*.

"Enlightenment" describes a natural consciousness and presence that is fully awakened to its own true nature. This liberation, as I'll explore in Part Three, feels like freedom, peace, and at times an irrepressible love without conditions. We deeply relax into life, and a way of being unfolds that does not feel at all personal. Rather than abandoning individual humanity, enlightenment is a lightening of it and includes compassion for the ways we become stuck in separateness.

Today's Spiritual Emergence

Transpersonal psychology uses "spiritual emergence" to describe a variety of phenomena that may arise through spiritual or energy practices. This term includes changes in consciousness and a variety of altered states, described throughout this book, to differentiate these anomalous events from pathological conditions. This all-inclusive category usually describes initiatory events that are the first movements in our journey to enlightenment.

Many young people experience spontaneous moments of awakening. One spiritual teacher observed that more and more young people, between the ages of fifteen and thirty, are showing up at her talks and reporting that they are familiar with the expansive experience of oneness, feel an intimate connection to the earth, and have gone through a spiritual awakening. Most have neither done a practice nor had a conscious longing for awakening.[2] Many spiritual teachers speculate that this is happening because we live in desperate times and need an influx of aware, creative, compassionate people who will actively serve others and contribute fresh ideas. This is a radical change from the traditional spiritual path of withdrawing from society and from the 1960s movements when young people felt a need to drop out of the mainstream to seek social alternatives.

There is currently a movement toward awakening evident in the abundance of inspirational books, experiential retreats, and organizational conferences—despite many cultural obstacles, distractions, and inadequate understanding. Ordinary people are waking up spontaneously and powerfully after exposure to teachings or practices, such as meditation and yoga, that they don't realize are designed to facilitate spiritual processes. Even popularized versions can change our body, breath, how our mind functions, our view of relationship, and our level of identification with conditioning.

A spiritual emergence, at any level, is an invitation to deepen our intention and open our mind and heart to the unfolding of an awakening process that will transform our relationship with life. We ask: "Could this happen to me?" "Does my heart long for truth?" "How can I invite awakening into my life?" "How can my awakening contribute to our world?"

From Suffering to Awakening

Just as there are many triggers for awakening, we also have predispositions to awaken that have been identified in the literature of mysticism. Today, we do not often call people who have experienced awakening "mystics," as it seems to be an old-fashioned term reserved for rare beings who lived in past centuries, like Catholic saints, Buddhas, Hindu gurus, Sufi dervishes, and Taoist sages. But when we read their stories, it's clear that their journeys as mystics usually began with struggles that are familiar to us. For hundreds of years, their recorded writings—whether nuns or poets, inspired teachers or artists—have described a division, or painful restlessness, within themselves prior to a moment of illumination when a great light or descent of grace fell upon them.

Some female mystics, including Saint Catherine of Genoa, Madame Guyon in France, and Anandamayi Ma in India, were married in the conventions of their times when marriages were determined by strict family edicts. They turned their passions toward a love of God, eventually becoming free from conditions that felt like imprisonment.

Men were often entangled in worldly finances, wars, and even revenge before they had awakenings that pulled them toward lives closer to nature and service. Saint Francis of Assisi, Saint Paul of Tarsus, and Milarepa the Tibetan saint are examples of the sudden transformation from fighter to spiritual seeker. Siddhartha was a wealthy prince and father, but when he saw suffering and death for the first time, he plunged dramatically into a spiritual search, leaving home to pursue truth and to become the enlightened Buddha. As a teenager, Ramana Maharshi suffered from profound grief and puzzlement after the deaths of both his father and then the uncle who had taken care of him. This suffering preceded his search and realization. Milarepa originally wanted yogic powers to gain revenge on an uncle who had stolen the family property, and after terrible consequences saw the evil in his heart and begged for liberation.

Today, many people who are awakening have histories of suffering, either physically or emotionally. Many among us were abused or neglected as children, experienced trauma or violence, or report chronic illness such as Lyme disease, environmental sensitivity, lupus, or chronic fatigue. Many endure emotional challenges, such as grief, depression, or anxiety, preceding a moment of breaking through into another dimension of consciousness.

One modern mystic, Eckhart Tolle, describes this experience clearly in his book *The Power of Now*. Until he was nearly thirty years old, Tolle says he lived in "a state of almost continuous anxiety interspersed with periods of suicidal depression." He writes that one morning he woke up with a feeling of absolute dread. "Everything felt so alien, so hostile, and so utterly meaningless that it created in me a deep loathing of the world. The most loathsome thing of all, however, was my own existence." Overwhelmed by this feeling, he longed for annihilation and thought "I can't live with myself any longer."

Suddenly, he realized how peculiar this thought was. For if there was an "I" who could not live with "myself," there must be two distinct things: the I and the self. "Only one of them could be real" he thought, and that stopped his mind.

> I was fully conscious, but there were no more thoughts. Then I felt drawn into what seemed like a vortex of energy. It was a slow movement at first and then accelerated. I was gripped by an intense fear, and my body started to shake. I heard the words "resist nothing," as if spoken by my chest. I could feel myself sucked into a void.[3]

After a while, the fear went away and he let himself fall. In the morning, Eckhart awakened to the sound of a bird and his entire sense of self was transformed, being full of wonder at the beauty and aliveness of the world. For the next five months, he lived in a state of peace and joy that gradually diminished, but eventually became his natural state. Journeying from despair into a transformed perspective, through energy, is common for many people who awaken without understanding or preparation.

Historically, seekers intentionally induced suffering to trigger awakening experiences. Long fasts and months of sitting in isolated caves are classical preparations for spiritual shifts. Buddhism and Christianity both emphasize impermanence and suffering as important motivations on the spiritual path, and some Indian mystical paths encourage direct rejection of all worldly pleasures. Ancient mystery schools even simulated a near-death experience (NDE) as a method of triggering transcendent experiences, as both NDE and the actual dying process can awaken us. However, not everyone's motivation for a spiritual search arises from a direct encounter with suffering.

Longing for Truth

Children can begin a spiritual journey by asking questions about the meaning of life, as they long to know what is true in a world of contradictions and to see beyond the veils of conventional religion or superficial values. Many scriptures suggest this longing arises from an unconscious, deeper part of self that wants to be remembered.

Some pursue this search through intellectual concepts and ideas for many years, but find that acquiring more and more knowledge does not lead to realization, although it can settle a mind that has a need to know. These great thinkers experience breakthroughs that take them beyond the horizontal learning curve of the intellect to expose the limitations of intellect in spiritual matters.

Our mind must expand beyond conceptual understanding. As we awaken, we can find complex, traditional, intellect-based ideas unsatisfying. So we bring our questions deep within ourselves, asking: "What am I?" "What is God?" or "Who am I?" Even with internal probing, we realize we cannot possibly know the answers through intellect alone. We need to embrace *not-knowing*. While questions like these may propel our spiritual emergence, our mind has no answers for them. We need to enter the unknown, to follow the inner curiosity and longing deep within our heart. Knowing the truth and feeling the spirit leap are kinesthetic and cellular, which is how awakening expands us into the unfamiliar territory of enlightenment.

Longing for Love

People who are inclined to follow their hearts may find that awakening comes in the midst of devotion, chanting, nature, or service. Classical Christian, Yogic, Buddhist, and Sufi approaches to awakening appeal to the heart. As a sincere devotee, we can fall into an unexpected and overwhelming love that drives us deeper into relationship with the cosmic self. Sufis call this awakening "coming home." We can sense our loving connection to a cosmic source by looking inward.

Realization can come on suddenly or evolve gradually, and there is no way of predicting how it will appear. But across cultures and centuries, we have the same realization. It can be described elaborately by saints and poets with terms like radiant emptiness, eternal expansion, unconditioned love, unbound consciousness, absolute oneness, ineffable joy, merging into the infinite, discovery of true nature, God-realization, and many other expressions. All of their attempts to put words to the awakening revelation are notably unable to describe the experience itself in a way another mind can grasp. This is because realization must be known directly and cannot be taught.

What Happens After an Awakening

What is predictable after an awakening or mystical insight is that the trajectory of our life is changed. We undergo a process of restructuring our energy, consciousness, and lifestyle.

This process can be chaotic, intense, and rock the spirit and body to its core. There may be moments of ecstasy beyond what we ever imagined possible, visions that lift our soul, an elimination of everything we ever believed was true, and the unfolding of great challenges and blessings. For a few, this happens simply, as a calm and radiant seeing that penetrates the small self, dissolves the seeker, and accepts life as it is. This feels like seeing something obvious that had been strangely overlooked. As a client named Jules told me:

> *The penny finally dropped that I am Consciousness, that only Consciousness exists, and that nothing is separate within Consciousness—making everything feel a bit like a dream. It feels so obvious now that I can't believe I never noticed it before.*

Often, we come back to earth with a thud. In some traditions, students are told the journey to enlightenment will take many lifetimes, or that attaining enlightenment is too advanced to even hope for in this life. All the student can do is live more peacefully, become devoted to service and practices, and be optimistic about the next life. So if students have an awakening that results from committed spiritual practices, they seldom report it. If they do, teachers commonly discount, dismiss, or misunderstand experiences—especially when erratic side effects are not discussed within the tradition.

When we talk about our realization, we can also be accused of being mentally ill or somehow pathological. The *masts*, the God-intoxicated madmen of India, may be people who have stumbled into awakening moments without the support needed to fulfill their promise.[4]

We can enter a gradual unfolding process that takes years and can be very challenging because of a lack of support and understanding. This feels like a slow, and often lonely, unraveling of our old sense of personal self. Eckhart Tolle was blessed by a stabilized feeling that followed his first awakening. Yet he still had to spend several years seeking to understand what had happened to him, and waiting to know what to do next with his life.

By boldly facing challenges that follow awakening, which I describe in depth in chapter 5, we can see them as unconscious elements needing to be recognized and released from our own psyches.

We can begin to clear their destructive and self-limiting tendencies. And as we awaken, our collective experience awakens. As the Buddha reportedly said, "When I woke up, the world woke up."

In the following chapters, you will read about the changes in energy and consciousness that occur during, and as a result of, spiritual awakening. I'll share the ways awakening impacts the minds, bodies, spirits, and lifestyles of modern spiritual seekers. Because many portals can send us into this mystery of knowing, I will share a wide range of reactions from people who enter this territory.

It is important to recognize both the challenges and great blessings of a spiritual journey. By bringing full respect and appreciation to this age-old evolution, we can move awakening out of the dark ages and into the modern world. We need to do this because it is a natural, human potential that offers greater clarity, wisdom, and peace to us personally, to the culture we live in, and to the earth as a whole.

2. Energy Moves Us Along the Way

In the West, spirituality has long been divorced from the activities of the physical body. Great efforts have been made to transcend the physical body, to control its desires and needs, and to achieve purity. As a result, the body's role in spiritual awakening is rarely discussed and our culture does not fully appreciate the potential of the body-mind connection. But if you are doing energy or healing practices, such as body therapy, breathwork, deep relaxation exercises, guided imagery, yoga, qigong, massage, or martial arts, you have likely felt the sensations of energy activating in your body. You may even have a sense that your body is a channel for moving energy. Here are two stories of awakening that happened suddenly, without any preparation or understanding.

Jimmy was a teenager when he did a very basic meditation for the first time, concentrating on his breath as it went in and out. A sudden blast of energy from the perineal region shot to the top of his head, like a cosmic orgasm with energy rushing as if through a fire hose.

> The sense of "I" dissolved in light, consciousness, and ecstasy.
> For how long, I do not know: seconds, minutes? When I came
> back, my heart was pumping like crazy and the whole
> experience cooled down in a few minutes.

Another young man named Joseph was in the second week of a meditation retreat when he felt a flow of energy all around his body and through his spine, along with tingling sensations and intense hot and cold rushes, movements, and uncontrollable shakings.

> Then I felt an explosion of energy in my brain and two days
> later a tsunami of energy came in through the top of my head,
> producing an astoundingly big expansion in consciousness that

seemed to encompass the whole universe. At this point I was
incredibly afraid and thought I was going to physically die.

These are descriptions of energy in motion. Have you ever thought of yourself as an energy field? Like everything in the world, we are made of atoms that are positively, negatively, or neutrally charged. That means we are all energy fields, vibrating entities that must have energy to exist. The formation of a fetus into a baby is an energetic phenomenon, and when the form and the energy reach full development, a child emerges into the world. Coming to life is an energetic activity, and so is dying. We can see that energy and con-sciousness simultaneously depart someone's body when he or she dies.

Everything within us is alive, moving and forming the physical-ity that holds a flow of consciousness. When we pursue spiritual or energetic practices, we can feel energy shifting, stirring, and even erupting. This is part of the awakening process, yet like Joseph we can become frightened and disoriented, as if we should not be experiencing it.

In some spiritual communities, energetic movement is consid-ered a distraction and an undesirable experience. Awakening energy may not be the goal of spiritual practice, but it is part of the journey. If all of life emerges through an energetic process, why should we be so worried when our transformation includes its movement?

In many Eastern traditions, our interior energy field is under-stood to be intimately related to the way our consciousness func-tions. Therefore, opening and harmonizing the flow of energy in our body gradually transforms our relationship to life by changing our consciousness. These shifts open our awareness to perceive new potentials and add new dimensions to our life. Anna, a psychothera-pist, went to see an acupressurist to release stiffness in her body. During the session, she found herself raising lots of energy and moving spontaneously.

I was shaking all over. The practitioner held a pressure point at
my coccyx and I went into a big vibration, a powerful wave of
energy sweeping up and through the top of my head. My upper

body felt swollen with energy. It was almost beyond my ability to endure and I flung to one side, moaning. I do not know if I blacked out or if it just stopped. Then I suddenly felt full of overwhelming love, intoxicated.

For several hours, Anna continued to feel throbbing and blissful energy flow all over her body, most intensely in her shoulders and head. She wanted to fall into this energy, to fly or swim in it, and never come back. For Anna, this was a transformative event that led to deeper emotional and meditative experiences.

I have often wondered why these sudden energetic shifts happen for some people, and yet so many do the same practice and never feel them. I meditated for fifteen years and it was not until I saw someone experiencing a breathwork session that I realized the link between spirituality and physical energy. I then experienced a session that connected my body to the stillness I had built in my mind through many years of meditation, released constricted energy, and activated kundalini. It is possible some bodies are simply more open, sensitive, and available to activation. Or perhaps there is a moment in our life, an optimal moment, in which an energetic opening can bring transformation.

James, an attorney, was a novice meditator attempting to reduce his work stress. On the third morning of his practice, he was surprised to feel energy arise from the pelvis.

It moved slowly through the center of my body all the way through my head with ecstatic sensations and inner lights and all the rest. It was very powerful. I had no idea what this experience was.

Similarly, we can have these opening experiences without any clue about what happened or why. Energetic openings can change our life. Energetic blocks in our body are felt as an uncomfortable physical contraction where energy is not moving freely, and they often hold the roots of a past emotional or physical trauma. They are most commonly felt in the stomach, back, and neck. The experience of releasing a block can be extremely blissful and permanently change how we relate with pain, physically and emotionally. When a block releases, we become more open and available to life.

Many practices we do to find inner calm or harmony also initiate awareness of, and movement in, this subtle energy system. So what is happening? Yogic perspectives of subtle energy offer a helpful aid to understanding. I have studied these extensively, and you will find many references to kundalini and the yogic subtle-body system in this book.

Universal Energy Moves Within Us

Beyond our personal experience, there is a cosmic force at work as universal energy moves within our body in unique ways that can trigger many sensations. According to the Indian treatise *Devatma Shakti: Divine Power:*

> Vedic philosophers regard the whole creation on physical and metaphysical planes as a play of different forces, all being different forms of one universal cosmic energy or power...the phenomenon may be compared with the formation of mists, clouds, lightning, thunder, rains, hail, snow, and so forth from an all-pervading atmosphere of vapor.[5]

In yoga, there is a cosmic energy within us known as *prana*. It enters a fetus at conception and becomes the bioenergy of life. A powerhouse of extra prana is coiled at the base of the spine and is known as *kundalini*. When kundalini is activated, it moves up through the body, bringing many physical, emotional, and psychic changes. It is often depicted, and referred to, as being like a snake. Some yoga practices are designed to awaken this transformative energy.

Chakras are energy centers located along our cerebral spinal system, and while they are not materially real, they are where yogis believe physical, subtle, and cosmic energies connect. The spot where kundalini coils is the chakra called *mooladhara*, which is located near the base of our spine. The energy of kundalini is considered an infinite, cosmic power that can transform consciousness.

It is the source of our life force, associated with sexual drive and procreation when coiled at the base. When awakened, kundalini can move either gradually or suddenly through the body, on its way through higher chakras to the top of the head, where it can connect with its source—the universal or cosmic energy. When we die, kundalini leaves the body and merges into this source.

Prana, the energy flow in our bodies, is commonly translated as "life force," and is not unique to yoga: it is called *chi* or *qi* in Chinese energy practices and *ki* in Japanese. Tantric Buddhist traditions recognize the role of energy in awakening, and advanced Sufi initiations activate it. Many indigenous cultures have rituals to arouse energy and create altered states through dance, drumming, and chanting. Ancient images of snakes and dragons have been associated with this potential for transformation by heightening energy and consciousness, which offered collective insight and healing for tribes. Some Charismatic Christian groups also heighten energy while speaking in tongues or moving ecstatically to music.

Around the world and for thousands of years, methods for sensing and harmonizing this life energy in the body have been used to improve health, increase longevity, and attain spiritual insight. Here are descriptions of some of them:

- Acupuncture and acupressure view the body based on an understanding that energy moves through channels called *meridians*, which is the basis for these healing techniques.

- A Jewish Kabbalist notes that: "Eventually you will reach an energy that is not in your control, rather your mind and thought are in its control."[6]

- Shakers and some Charismatic Christians have practices that trigger involuntary movements and shaking.

- Subud is a spiritual community originating in Indonesia that opens to the divinely inspired, spontaneous expression of energy.

⊛ Yogic practices may trigger a "pranic release" that manifests as involuntary shaking.

⊛ Huna is an ancient Hawaiian system designed to activate the life force.

⊛ Somatic therapy, an evolving practice in Western psychotherapy, has introduced methods of shaking, tapping, and working with breathing practices to release old patterns of trauma held in the body.

Many people do not want a defined spiritual path, and others engage spiritual practices with Buddhist, Christian, Sufi, or Shamanic orientations that are quite different from the yogic one. For some people, a complete immersion into the yogic understanding, practices, and lifestyle may be a life calling. I find most Westerners are not inclined this way.

In my work with clients, I have come to value how the yogic perspective offers some understanding of why the unique experiences that arise on their spiritual journeys happen. I don't rely heavily on an understanding of the routes that kundalini takes, preferring to focus on the emotional and lifestyle changes that support spiritual realization. At the same time, I have found it is useful to be aware of how kundalini and the chakras work, because they convey some universal conditions and potentials in spiritual experience.

A View of How Awakening Energy Moves

In yogic science, the foundation of our energy field is at the base of the spine, where kundalini is said to be wound 3.5 times. Our central energy channel in the spine is called *sushumna*. When kundalini awakens, it optimally will move through sushumna and begin to impact the chakras—although in some systems it is believed to take other routes in channels that are less useful for a full awakening.[7] I have never seen an explanation for why kundalini would choose one channel over another, but teachers do say this is why a knowledgeable guide and proper preparation are needed before activation.

Most yogic texts describe 72,000 lines of energy called *nadis* that flow from the primary chakras, which I will soon describe. Nadis are invisible tube-like threads of subtle ethereal matter through which consciousness, intelligence, sensation, and emotion flow. Swami Sivananda writes "They are not physical, measurable, dissectable structures within our physical body, but are the basic energies which underlie and motivate life and consciousness."[8] Kundalini science describes six possible nadis through which an activated kundalini may move: *brahma, chitrini, lakshmi, vajra, saraswati,* and *sushumna.* They each have unique impacts, with risings that may be partial, intermediate, or complete. I'll explore their effects a bit.

- **Brahma nadi** offers a sudden, direct, and complete route to realization that is extremely rare.

- **Chitrini nadi** is a path that moves energy through the chakras very gradually, opening blocks along the way.

- **Lakshmi nadi** is a channel to the right of sushumna that is dangerous to open, said to bring great heat, fire, and trauma.

- **Vajra nadi** movement is considered a deflected arising that may open a person to special talents, such as paranormal abilities, or trigger intense sexual drive, and restlessness, but does not lead to realization—instead it may cause energetic depletion and psychological disturbances.

- **Saraswati nadi** movement brings intermittent experiences of oneness, creativity, heightened spirituality, mental clarity, intuition, and even paranormal experiences, but the intense energy can also trigger hormonal and digestive issues.

- **Sushumna nadi** is considered optimal, as its movement is gradual and more stable as it moves through and intensifies various chakras, bringing transformation.

In this system, the remedy for a problematic kundalini arising is to reroute the energy back to the sushumna nadi. This can be difficult, because it requires the release of certain energetic blockages, and you must have strong vital energy and a focused mind.[9]

In its coiled state, kundalini seems to hold the system in an energetic stasis. Some tantric and yoga schools intentionally activate kundalini so that it rises. This fosters awakening experiences that stimulate a deconstructing, rewiring, and reorganizing of the energy field. As it enlivens chakra areas, energy spreads out and intensifies movement through the nadis, thousands of which branch out from the central channel. The impact of this heightened energy promotes the release of old patterns and an opening to new perceptions and experiences. When we experience a block, or great discomfort in some area of our body, from a yogic perspective a chakra may need to be activated and awakened.

Some Types of Energy That Are Activated

Practices such as yogic breathing, chanting, and concentration rely on the chakras as focal points to assist awakening by clearing and transforming energy, which make our energy field more open and our body more flexible. Each chakra is in an area of the body that holds unique blockages and conditions that can be released. Some people are born with an open chakra that supports unique capacities or talents, such as strong compassion or extraordinary creativity or charismatic speaking.

There are many books written about chakras, and this can be confusing because each presents a unique perspective though the differing theories of traditions and individuals. There are a variety of interpretations, and occultists, mystics, and yogis have divergent points of view. Swami Satyananda Saraswati wrote that our personal visions of chakras may vary in terms of color and interpretation according to personal tendencies, which may account for varying approaches. I will provide only limited descriptions.

I was told by Baba Hari Das, an Ashtanga Yoga master, that there are fifty chakras in the body, but there are six or seven all along sushumna that are most commonly known. Some esoteric traditions speak of multiple chakras above the head. Surgeons may identify chakras with nerve fibers gathered in various plexuses, and a clairvoyant may see their colors and movement.[10] Some people view them as symbolic, not literally existing, but clairvoyants say they can see them spinning like wheels and feel them radiating. In some styles of yogic thought and practice, there are elaborate images for the major chakras with colors, deities, and symbols that have specific meanings. A symbolic opening, or turning over, of a lotus can represent the flowering of a person's potential.

I have chosen to describe the chakras through the portal of the kundalini tantra lineage taught by Swami Satyananda Saraswati, and to emphasize some of the experiences associated with each chakra that clients have reported to me. According to the kundalini tantra tradition, these are the major chakras.

Mooladhara: Root or Foundation

This chakra is located at the base of the spine. Mooladhara chakra is considered the seat of guilt, complexes, and passions. It is the foundation for a sense of being in our body. When it first awakens, we might feel explosive emotions and a sensation that our body is floating in space. Once kundalini is activated here, yogis believe it is important to move energy through it as quickly as possible.

Swadhisthana: Dwelling Place

Slightly above mooladhara, at the level of the coccyx or tailbone, is the chakra related to the reproductive and urinary systems. It is also involved in the initial awakening of kundalini. When kundalini energy is stuck here, we may experience many negative emotions, sexual fantasies, lethargy, depression, and other forms of inner turmoil. Sexual energy can become intense. As life force energy, kundalini stays active in this chakra area during adulthood, stimulating sexual drive and procreation. Because sexual release involves a downward flow of energy, and kundalini yoga practices are designed to reverse this energy upward, sexual activity is discouraged in many yogic traditions. However in some tantric traditions known as "left-handed traditions," sexual stimulation, within an elaborate ritual with a trained and awakened initiator, can be used as a method for igniting and raising kundalini.[11] Some people describe the bliss of an initial arising of kundalini as feeling like a whole-body orgasm.

Manipura: City of Jewels or Jeweled Lotus

In Buddhist traditions that work with subtle energies and in many tantric texts, kundalini is said to awaken from the manipura chakra. By using it as the starting point, awakening energy is believed to be in no danger of receding back into the lower chakras. Manipura is behind the naval, on the inner wall of the spinal column, and is considered the center of dynamism, energy, will, and achievement. It is said to radiate energy throughout our body. When it is deficient, we feel lifeless, lack vitality, and may be depressed. When it is weak, psychological issues may arise such as low self-esteem or discouragement, as well as physical problems like indigestion. When the chakra is strong and awake, we feel empowered to move forward in our life. If mind and heart are not awakened, we might feel a strong sense of purpose that is driven by ego demands. If we are awakening, we may have an authentic, intuitive sense of being in alignment with what is right for us.

Anahata: Unstruck or Unbeaten

This name comes from the unbroken beat of our heart. The chakra is located directly behind the center of the chest. It is believed to be responsible for all the creative sciences and fine arts. When it first awakens, we may hear voices or music from other realms, buzzing and humming sounds, and the music of a flute. It is a center of wish-fulfillment, so when this is awakened, yogis are often warned to avoid negative thoughts and people, and to focus on positive thoughts to empower decision-making and strengthen their sense of will. Sometimes we feel our heart has broken open, through love or grief, and it can be painful when old wounds are released. Sensitivity may become acute. Most of us have some blockage in this area because of grief, anger, loss, and disappointment. When the heart awakens, these will fall away—a significant turning point in the awakening process. Afterward, we can experience a spontaneous, unconditional love for all beings. Devotional practices in all traditions aim at opening the heart.

Vishuddha: Purification

This chakra is located in the cervical plexus, directly behind the pit of the throat. When awakened, it is associated with eloquence, self-expression, wisdom, compassion, freedom from depression, and peace of mind. It is associated with reading the thoughts of others both near and far, and with longevity. We commonly feel blockages in the throat chakra due to the many ways we have learned to withhold free expression and keep quiet in the face of difficult situations. I believe it is also associated with creativity, as I have found in my own experience that when my mind veers off into possible writing projects during meditation, I can feel energy active in my throat. If I move this energy, the thoughts stop.

Ajna: Command Center or Guru Center

Because this chakra is directly between the eyes and slightly above them, and because it is associated with psychic seeing, it is often called a "third eye." In kundalini yoga, this is the chakra that links our mind to the guru, or that enables us to hear the voice of an inner guru or guide. It is also the area where we might feel nothingness or meet the void, as ego drops away. It may also open us to astral and psychic dimensions of experience, including sounds, visions, and light. When we see stunning, bright light, it is likely kundalini is active here. Yogic teachings describe various levels of this chakra's awakening, including seeing the light of one-thousand moons, and later, one-thousand suns.

Sahasrara: One Thousand

This is not considered a chakra in every kundalini system. The number 1,000 represents access to the infinite. Some systems describe it as located at the top of the head, and others place it above the head. It represents the culmination of the awakening process, when the sense of individuality fades and consciousness awakens to itself. It signifies the dissolution into *samadhi,* union with the divine. Swami Saraswati calls its full experience the "void of totality" and the "unfolding of enlightenment."[12]

With this brief description of the chakras, we have explored how some classical yogic traditions recognize that various experiences arise during a transformative process on the way to enlightenment. The Resources section of this book and also my website list a variety of books that offer more detailed descriptions and interpretations of chakras and our subtle body system. I'll continue to refer to chakras throughout the book.

Living with Energy

As we awaken, life force energy moves through us to clear out old traumas, beliefs, and barriers that are woven in our body's energetic structure. This works similarly to a move from one home to another, with serious downsizing. When we're getting ready to move, we sort our stuff, clean out the cupboards, discard whatever we don't need, and get rid of items that are too bulky to bring with us. Doing this makes room for a new life in a new home, which has different dimensions and different needs that we must meet.

In a similar way, to shift into a new way of being the energetic body gets cleared out and reorganized, and whatever is no longer needed gets discarded. Kundalini transforms these old patterns so that we can see clearly again, free of conditioned responses, and become open to compassion, love, and expression that is authentic. As I'll describe more in the next chapter, energetic transformation supports the movement of consciousness into awareness of vastness and connection with its source. For this to happen, all our identifications become irrelevant.

Changes in energy can feel chaotic—even more so if our conditioning is traumatic, our mind does not understand what is happening, our body is full of toxins from stress or unhealthy food, or if the change occurs with psychedelic substances or plant medicines. This is why, in ancient times, people did not pursue awakening until their physical bodies were relatively pure and their lifestyle was managed within the simple confines of an ashram, cave, or forest retreat. And their transformation processes happened through solo or community rituals with experienced teachers or elders at hand to offer guidance and help.

Today we tend to enter the awakening process with many unhealthy beliefs, conditions, and injuries that need to be released. We are part of a culture that considers awakening unnatural, or even dangerous, because the results take us beyond mainstream concepts about divinity, achievement, and worldly success. An awakened person does not fit in as comfortably as conventional people wish them to. For example, upon awakening we might watch news reports and feel that most of the world is tragically insane. We might realize that our friends and families are entangled in personal stories or beliefs that are imaginary but cause them great pain.

While our general culture and some spiritual teachers consider energy unreal, nonexistent, or irrelevant to the awakening experience, I consider it to be a natural occurrence. Energy may arise suddenly or gradually, softly or intensely, create emotional upheaval or bliss—our life-force movements vary as much as our life histories. This is a spiritual birthing process, and sometimes it is as messy as our physical birth was. There may be pain or exhaustion involved, and it may be necessary to diagnose, or rule out, medical conditions because an underlying illness or hormonal imbalance can be aggra-vated by energy arising. These are all challenges we can face, which I discuss in depth in Part Two.

Because energy is intimately linked with consciousness, when we meet these movements with curiosity, openness, and patience—instead of fear—the energy uncoils to support a consciousness that remembers its true nature. As energy arises, it often triggers shifts in consciousness that ultimately promote spiritual realization. In the following chapter, we'll look at the awakening of consciousness.

3. Consciousness Recalls Its Essence

S cientists cannot agree on what consciousness is and consider it a mystery of the brain. Most brain researchers do not explore the nature of consciousness and many consider it a puzzle beyond inter-pretation. Those who have tried to understand it researched con-sciousness by examining how various brain areas store information and work together to produce a sense of self. A few pioneers, inspired by ancient teachings and modern reports, are currently exploring the possibility that consciousness is primary in existence, suggesting we are in consciousness rather than consciousness being in us. Viewing consciousness as the primary source of life would change the basis of our perspective of human psychology and physiology.

Vedanta is a Hindu philosophy that says all of creation arises out of one source, which morphs into various forms or appearances, cre-ating billions of various experiences and experiencers. Many people who report mystical and transcendent awakenings sense this to be true. When I look at the phenomena reported by my clients, despite the variety, they support this model of consciousness. This is how it works: one infinite and universal source becomes, or is primarily, consciousness; its vibration creates the building blocks of life; it then experiences itself as energy. We are each one form of the energy field created by this infinite consciousness, with our breath allowing this energy to be in continual flow.

In the *Upanishads*, sacred texts at the core of Vedanta teachings, descriptions of the experience of awakening evoke the ocean. They say the ocean is like the fullness of our universal nature, and our personal consciousness is like a wave arising from it. Without the ocean there would be no waves. Even as our individual awareness arises like a wave, we can never lose our essence as part of the vast consciousness of the whole, as each wave eventually recedes back into the ocean. Sivananda Saraswati uses this analogy to help students understand the relation of our true nature to the source and substance of all existence.

> There are countless waves rolling in the vast ocean. Each wave is distinguished from the other and each wave can be perceived separately, one by one. But all are water only, and are not separate from the great ocean. All are one only in reality. The difference is only apparent…they are perceived to be separate from one another.[13]

Writers throughout history have used the ocean as a metaphor for consciousness. Taoist teacher Lao Tzu wrote that "Tao in the world is like a river, flowing home to the sea."[14] Taoism encourages going with the flow, not trying to swim upstream, because it is by following the natural flow of life that harmony can be found. The turning of consciousness inward and resting it in our center is like water in the poetry of Taoism, as compared to the fire of our outward interactions.[15]

Consciousness and Shifts of Identity

A sense of separation troubles many of us, as we long to feel connected, to know our "tribe," or to return to a sense of being at home—even without knowing where that is. This can lead to a spiritual search, because we feel a sense of emptiness inside when we do not know our origin as universal consciousness.

We are aware because consciousness exists. The sensations we feel in our body—touching, hearing, seeing, smelling, tasting—are known because embodied consciousness notices them. Likewise, our thoughts and emotions can be observed by consciousness in its role as awareness. The sense that "I am this person" is felt because there is consciousness in the body. Over time, we collected a set of experiences and opinions that we identify with as our separate and unique self. We hope our uniqueness will always endure.

However, this unique self is not as stable as we think it is. In an awakening event, it can feel as if it is dissolving, possibly because energy is moving through new patterns in our brains. In fact, many who report awakenings have felt vibrations, crawling sensations, and other disturbances in their heads, saying it feels as if their brains were being rewired.

Current brain research suggests that there are specific areas of the brain responsible for conscious functioning and self-awareness. If those areas are not active, as in a coma, then we are not acting as a separate "me." Other factors, such as damage to certain areas of the brain, or the use of psychedelic substances, can produce a loss of identification with our sense of personal self. So can prolonged meditation. Andrew Newberg, MD, and Mark Waldman have done extensive neurological studies looking at brain activity in people who have had awakenings. They found that initially meditation produces increased activity in the frontal and parietal lobes, and this is correlated with reduced emotional intensity, as well as feeling grounded and centered. This activity does not lead to enlightenment; however, when there is a sudden and substantial decrease in activity in the frontal and parietal lobes of the brain, the response is a loss of control (surrender), the weakening or disappearance of the sense of self, and a dramatic increase of emotion. They have seen these patterns in brain-scan studies with spiritually awakened people and believe this is when "profound insights associated with enlightenment begin to enter consciousness."[16] These neurological studies suggest why we may sit in meditation or prayer in a peaceful, inner calm for years, then suddenly explode into a dramatic shift of perception and oneness with the universe. Joy was a longtime meditator who had a spontaneous shift while walking out of her kitchen.

> I fell to my knees as some kind of explosion took place, rushing up through me, as if a match had been lit in a space filled with gas. After a long, silent moment, the thought came: "I don't know what I'm doing." After that, it was a merging with everything, which produced a constant feeling so intense and joyful that I thought at times it would kill me. But I didn't care.

*The experience taught me that there is a real, specific meaning
to the word "ecstasy." It far, far outstripped any other experience
I have known, including falling in love and sex. Which is the
real predicament. It was like a drug I could not get a supply of.
In peak moments, when I was sitting in meditation, which I did
for hours a day, I could feel some kind of energy pouring down
into my head, solid, almost like a pillar. It was made up of
brilliant white sparks of some kind that splashed into rainbow
colors all around. I would nearly lose consciousness, then come
back to myself, often with tears pouring down my face.*

When consciousness awakens itself spontaneously, our body-
mind system eventually tends to respond by reaffirming the positions, concepts, and attachments with which we previously identified.
So even though we have glimpsed the truth, we must go through a
period of continually choosing: truth, freedom, and realization
versus re-identification with our old mental and physical assumptions. We go back and forth, progress and fall back into old ways of
being. We experience our self as coming in and out of awakening
because we are entangled in a false sense of self. This choosing may
take a short time or a long time. It may feel like a process. In some
way, we are all in this process, in a continuum between being caught
in our mental projections about our separate self and separate others,
and being present and open, free of all projections.

Ways to Know Consciousness

One way to understand how our consciousness operates is to consider these four levels of experiencing consciousness.

- ✿ We can be unconscious, as in sleep, where consciousness rests and we are unaware of any sense of "I."

- ✿ We can function through our conditioned consciousness that holds all our experiences, beliefs, and patterns
  of thought attached to the sense of "I" or "me."

- We may have moments of pure awakened consciousness, free of "me" conditioning and more spontaneously responsive in the moment.

- A fourth level, known as *turiya* in Vedanta, is present in deep sleep and in samadhi when awareness is merged in the source of consciousness.

During waking hours, the content of the unconscious influences our moods and behavior but the "I" is not identified with it, so we are unaware of its impact on our lives. As we move through the day, we function from our I-identity, so our thoughts label, divide, and objectify the world. We make decisions, assumptions, and judgments according to our personal beliefs, desires, and aversions, all influenced by our history and past experiences. These influences of the unconscious cloud pure, awakened consciousness just as storm clouds can darken the bright spaciousness of the sky. So they must be cleared before true liberation is possible.

Father Thomas Keating, the founder of Contemplative Outreach and the Centering Prayer movement, addresses the mental disturbances that may occur in contemplative practice and calls these the unloading of the unconscious.

> Emotionally charged thoughts are the chief way that the unconscious has of expelling chunks of emotional junk. In this way, without your perceiving it, a great many emotional conflicts that are hidden in your unconscious and affecting your decisions more than you realize are being resolved. As a result, over a period of time you will feel a greater sense of well-being and inner freedom. The very thoughts that you lament while in prayer are freeing the psyche from the damage that has accumulated in your nervous system over a lifetime.[17]

Therapists and spiritual teachers who work with spiritual emergence recognize the value of facing and accepting these conflicts and issues if one is to progress in the spiritual unfolding process.

Occasionally we feel moments of pure, awakened consciousness— free of conditioned thought—and we are fully present without separation. This may happen during meditation when the mind chatter stops, when we feel a silent and deep state of intimacy with life and nature, or in a crisis demanding our full attention and immediate response. Awakened consciousness responds from an immediacy that is unaffected by personal history. It is intuitive, spontaneous and direct. Awakened, pure consciousness exists before and continues beyond personal identifications. In this state, we may:

- ⊛ have multi-dimensional experiences and also see the simplest creation, like a flower or a child, as wondrous and miraculous;

- ⊛ know ourselves as profound stillness; and

- ⊛ sense presence without any attachment to the one who is present; it is something that has always been with us, but we have been unaware of it because of the many distractions of the mind and emotions.

Consciousness can wake up under many circumstances. Before and after an awakening, many of us experience a state that is free of ego, as if there is no "me." It is a sense of vastness and space, which is commonly described as *emptiness*. Emptiness can cause us to feel lost and ungrounded because the sense of "I" is gone, but this emptiness is pregnant with potential. Releasing ego-identity is essential as consciousness becomes ready to realize the truth of itself.

The Egolessness of Emptiness

Our human mind is used to being busy: it sorts, divides, judges, maintains our separate identity, and relates to social constructs with which it either identifies or rebels against. If our consciousness slips out of thoughts, even for just a few moments, we can discover there is nothing for our mind to hang on to. When consciousness is experiencing itself as presence, at first awareness may feel like empty space. In this emptiness, we experience freedom and openness to unknown possibilities.

In a spiritual sense, falling into emptiness comes in the aftermath of losing the sense of a personal self, even temporarily. Our sense of being a separate self is actually very fragile. Just as our identity now is quite different from what it was when we were ten years old, it continues to morph depending on what we are doing, how we look and feel physically, how we are treated by others, and even what someone else is saying about us. This sense of self is felt in our tendency to want to appear a certain way, to be acceptable as we are, and to defend our rights and positions to our self and to others. It drives beliefs, desires, and emotions. All these activities in our consciousness sustain our separate sense of being someone who is unique and special. It does not matter if an identity is positive or negative, our thoughts and emotions attempt to hold on to it. This "me" that we have developed, and try to maintain, is the part of us we most fear losing when we die.

When we feel existential emptiness, when this identification has slipped away—and we are in a place of total stillness, darkness, or vastness—we can feel shocked. And after the experience fades, we can feel stunned, depleted, and afraid. Clara, a teacher and long-term meditator, experienced this.

> While in retreat, after a meditation it felt like the bottom dropped out of existence. Suddenly, there was only complete emptiness, darkness, nothingness. It was utter and complete emptiness, nothingness. Black. Without boundaries or distinctions. Then these little, bubble-like formations began to emerge out of the nothingness. Each little bubble appeared to be a word. More bubbles became what seemed like more words strung together. It felt like DNA was emerging. There was only some sort of awareness happening. When my mind kicked in, it felt like this was the nothingness from which everything arises. It was so empty that it was scary to me. As I became aware and started to sense my body, I thought I might fall out of my chair. I kept thinking to myself "The body knows what to do."

Emptiness can feel like a dark night of the soul, as described by Saint John of the Cross,[18] because it is disorienting for the egoic self, which strives hard to keep us identified with our roles, emotions, and thoughts. But once we understand the nature of emptiness, we may fall in love with it, and then become it.

The Mystical Experience of Nothingness

Emptiness is recognized by mystics of every culture. Daniel Matt reveals teachings from Kabbalah that describe the depth of primordial being as "boundless."

> Because of its concealment from all creatures above and below, it is also called nothingness. If one asks, "What is it?" the answer is "Nothing," meaning no one can understand anything about it. It is negated of every conception.[19]

The great German mystic Meister Eckhart called this emptiness "the desert of the Godhead where no one is at home." His disciple, Dominican friar John Tauler, describes this emptiness as

> All *there* is so still and mysterious and so desolate: for there is nothing there but God only, and nothing strange...This wilderness is the quiet desert of the Godhead, into which He leads all who are to receive this inspiration of God, now or in eternity.[20]

In a classic work on Christian spirituality, Evelyn Underhill called this place one "which is to the intellect emptiness, but to the heart a fulfillment of all desire." She describes the ecstasies of mystics as consciousness merging with overwhelming spaciousness in moments when all attention to the outside senses and experiences is fully withdrawn. This moment is the attainment of "pure being," or the moment in which God is met and known in nothingness. It is considered the goal of true contemplation.[21]

Ironically one of the Christian arguments against Buddhism is its emphasis on emptiness, suggesting an unconscious bias, or misunderstanding, about the direct experience of what the mystics say is God. Because in Buddhism, emptiness represents the fundamental nature of all things, all thought, all experience.

As a Buddhist meditator begins to perceive the illusionary world of the mind as empty, insubstantial, and transitory, consciousness becomes more and more available in its true essence. This opens up to a realization of Buddha nature, which the mystics experience as divine.

Frances Bennett, a former Trappist monk who blends Christian mysticism, Buddhism, and Vedanta in his teachings, points directly to the potential of emptiness in spiritual awakening when he says,

> Another way of describing the spacious awareness that is sometimes called "emptiness" is to refer to it as "unconditional openness." I have taken to calling it that because this phrase seems to point a bit better to its essence which, for me, is LOVE.

I find that when I read the poetic and joyful descriptions of experiences of emptiness, my own mind resonates, vibrates, and opens into a subtle bliss I cannot describe. True scriptures, read in miniscule doses, can speak directly to our senses and soothe the fears of our overcautious mind.

Forms Within Emptiness

To understand our true nature, consciousness must take a journey that reveals all that we are not. For most of us who long to know God, or to know what is true, this is a long inner journey in which our shadowy sides, stuck points of view, traumas, and emotional contractions appear to be faced and released. Consciousness enters the vastness of emptiness in which there is no-self, that is, no personal self—just one cosmic self, one consciousness penetrating all existence. Some of us feel this to be God, some feel it to be our true nature, and we resolve to deepen our awakening. Our mind becomes filled with questions such as:

Why am I having these odd experiences and what do they mean?

What am I supposed to do with this?

Am I losing my mind? Or ill? Or dying?

What does this sense of nothingness have to do with God?

What do I tell my family is happening to me?

Am I enlightened? What is going to happen next?

How do I align my life or work with this knowing?

Why did this happen to me? What is life asking of me?

Our thinking mind is not big enough to grasp the whole of our journey to enlightenment. It has created models, like yoga science, Buddhist insights, and esoteric practices, but these do not convey the essence. We might understand the chemistry of water, but that is not the same knowing of water as drinking it when we are thirsty.

This limitation of thought calls us to rest instead in this unconditional openness, allowing it to permeate the cells of our body. When a heart embraces this emptiness, it becomes possible to bring unconditional compassion and love into the world. Here is the way emptiness is described by a Western man, who was once a Buddhist monk.

The vastness is right there, so apparent, so full, and so clear. I know that the nothingness and the everything are who I am, god arising, and emptiness manifesting in this moment, bursting into form. Who I am is the point that is happening, moment after moment. The living of that is the question.

In the next chapter, we will look at the many portals through which we can be invited to awaken and eventually live an awakened life. Perhaps one of them is already very familiar to you.

4. The Many Portals of Awakening

I have been blessed by encountering remarkable people with the courage to share their awakening stories with the world and to be unique individuals. Their experiences don't fit today's mainstream religious beliefs or psychological paradigms. This growing subculture of truth-seekers is expanding perspectives on what the potential of human consciousness is. Their stories reveal many portals that initiate awakening and transformation, mentally, emotionally, physically, and spiritually.

I honor each portal as a gateway to awakening, as we are all called to different paths. When we enter a portal, we can experience energy arising and consciousness opening in ways that expand our perception of reality. As part of this expansion, we may find ourselves releasing habitual ways of thinking, repressed patterns, uncomfortable memories, and darker shadow material from the unconscious. This may be accompanied by the challenges described in the next chapter, and perhaps they are why most spiritual traditions include practices to develop clarity, compassion, and unconditional love. When these qualities have been developed, it is easier for us to witness the darkness, or the failings in ourselves and others, with wisdom and compassion for the human condition. We can witness our inner experiences, whether negative or positive, more dispassionately.

In my experience, this kind of preparation is rare. Instead, when portals awaken unconscious material, both teachers and students are shocked. Both can be unaware that we all carry shadows in our unconscious. Teachers don't know how to deal with these issues and find them disturbing. They are often suppressed. In this chapter, I share descriptions of awakening within common and uncommon portals. Culturally, we are generally taught to acknowledge only one reality: that which can be proven in a factual and material way. This limited definition of reality greatly inhibits our openness, wisdom, and understanding about human wellness and potential. This is unfortunate for the culture as a whole, but it can be disastrous for any of us who are misunderstood, judged, or labeled mentally ill as a result of an awakening. It can hinder a radiant, highly productive, peaceful life. My hope is that when you read about how others have experienced a portal you engage, you will better understand your own awakening events.

Meditation

Meditation may, or may not, be a religious practice. Eastern spiritual communities see it as a way to realize our true nature. Some Western traditions cultivate an inner connection with God through meditation. Other groups meditate to induce altered states of awareness and mystical experience. And many people today use basic forms of it—such as mindfulness or vipassana—to improve health and well-being, calm body and mind, and evoke serenity and clarity.

Research indicates that meditation increases neuroplasticity and balancing in brain structures, which improve resilience, integration, inner harmony, and functioning.[22] The practices are shown to be so beneficial that some corporations are recommending it to their employees. A 2012 survey found that 8 percent of adults in the United States, or 18 million people, practice meditation.[23] Many people who do it ask and receive nothing more than the abundant practical benefits. As the health needs of an over-stressed society increase, the mental, physical, and emotional benefits of meditation attract many people unfamiliar with its spiritual potential. They may be unaware that, for thousands of years, meditation has been a method for awakening energy and transforming consciousness.

Even if it's not our intention, when we practice meditation awakening may occur. By aligning our energy and quieting our mind, we clear debris from our unconscious. Entering into the stillness of meditation can answer existential questions, including matters of life and death. It can open our heart, bringing bliss and peace, and it can activate energies that produce major changes.

Meditation offers a great foundation for awakening, but not all meditation is the same. Over the centuries, various methods have evolved that have different styles of entering deep truths and altering our consciousness. The methods effectively address the variety of personality types and cultural patterns, and what works well for one person may not fit well for another. Although most traditions discourage moving from one school to another, in the beginning some experimentation may help us find a practice and a community that suit us well.

During meditation practice, we quiet thoughts and relax physical impulses. This encourages concentration and contemplation, and offers periods of time with no outer distraction from inner experience. When we are in meditation, we withdraw from the world but a lot happens all the same. If we focus on a chakra area, such as the heart or third eye, energies can activate that produce unfamiliar sensations as the chakra is cleared. If we sit in stillness and allow everything to be as it is, we eventually stabilize peace and relaxation so we can apply them in everyday life. With no resistance to what is, we can experience profound freedom.

We can also experience disturbances. We can feel habitually fidgety, anxious, and overwhelmed by our own thoughts. Serena, a Zen practitioner, shares a story of energetic movement during a group meditation retreat, a setting that couldn't cope with her awakening process.

> My initial experience was very pleasant, with the sensation of energy flowing up my body from my lower back, accompanied by bliss and an internal vision of radiance. But then my body began shaking and twisting, my arms flapping. I gasped as these energies shook me, but none of the movements were painful. Eventually my teacher asked me to stop meditation. Another student who was a doctor of Chinese medicine said I could be endangering my health, and the students in general seemed to be alarmed or annoyed at my process.

As I described in chapter 2, kundalini movement like Serena describes can be a part of the spiritual process. She knew the movements were just part of the spiritual process, rather than evidence of psychosis or danger, so she was unafraid. But the reaction in the group eventually led Serena to lose her connection with a community that could have been an important support. This lack of understanding leads many students to separate from their spiritual companions. We can feel isolated and worried about our process, just at the point when our awakening is deepening.

If you realize that your process during meditation may disturb others, limit attendance at meditation retreats unless you are clear that the teacher can accept your activity. Consult with the teacher and explain your situation. Some retreats allow you to spend a few sessions alone in your room or walking in nature, times when you can balance, harmonize, and integrate. When we are not afraid of our process and understand it, teachers may be less reactive and help us arrange our retreat participation in supportive ways. For example, meditating with our eyes slightly open can reduce some inner phenomena. We can learn to use awareness to go into energy experiences, then come back out again. Because once we know how to go into a meditative state deliberately, we also know the pathway out of it. This gives us the option of stopping a disturbing incident while meditating in a group.

Movement

People begin movement practices like yoga, qigong, tai chi, and martial arts seeking flexibility, better balance and strength, calmness and centeredness, and generally healthier lives. A consistent movement practice improves and sustains good health, and most practitioners in the West never pursue the deeper philosophy that sustains these traditions. These practices have been developed in places like India, China, Indonesia, and the Middle East to activate spiritual awakening by directly impacting the subtle body energy field. They are portals to awakening energy and consciousness.

When we combine them with a sincere meditation practice, they can make us even more available to the grace of realization.

Yoga Practice

In 2016, more than 36 million people were practicing yoga in the United States.[24] Yoga is best known in the West as a physical practice of postures, or *asanas*, that improve flexibility and health. When done simply as a great physical exercise, asanas are less likely to stimulate spiritual awakening, but they will create a physical body better able to navigate the changes should our spirit leap.

The word *yoga* is Sanskrit and means "to yoke," which evokes what the system is ultimately about—connecting our body-mind with its source. Classical yoga uses asanas to activate and direct the energies of the subtle body toward awakening. They open the flow of energies within the body, breaking through blocks and opening them up. When combined with breathing practices, they become even more powerful methods for transforming the body, both within and without. Advanced yoga practices are designed to:

- activate latent kundalini energy curled at the base of the spine;

- bring it up through the body;

- encourage it to enter the chakras, each of which denotes an ascending level of consciousness[25];

- catalyze a process of turning over chakras to release old, conditioned patterns and blocks;

- and lead us into samadhi as we merge with universal consciousness.

Many people are familiar with the seven major chakras and some do yoga practices, offered in classes or on the Internet, to transform them. Yogis continuously work with the chakras to overcome challenges and issues carried from this life and previous lives.

Chakras are said to be spinning vortices that move energies. When we clear them, yogis speculate that chakra energy is converted from higher realms to be used in our physical world. New capacities can blossom, and we no longer function from the contracted patterns previously held in that chakra. Our energy moves upward.

As our body learns to be open to energy flows, kundalini may arise and move through the head and upper chakras. This impacts and possibly reorganizes many areas of the brain, which enables us to feel consciousness in its most pure and elemental form. If this happens, there is a possibility of awakening to our true nature and living with deep peace. In this way, yoga science provides a model for a disciplined process of kundalini awakening that facilitates transformation.[26]

Most yoga teachers, whether teaching in a gym or studio, are not familiar with this science or its details. Many have called me for help after a surprising and intense awakening of their own. Often there are subtle hints of this unfolding even before kundalini arises: as described in chapter 2, there can be energy releases, tingling at the base of the spine or in the third eye, ripples of pleasure, or heat arising in the body. Sometimes there is even a sudden rising of energy from our base through our crown, even when kundalini has not activated. In classical yoga, these are called *prana tattva*, "energy movement." Cheryl was travelling in Southeast Asia when she went to Thailand to attend a monthlong asana course, with no background at all in the tradition.

We were practicing six hours a day and the synchronicities kept unfolding. They illustrated every spiritual book I'd read, and all the dots were connecting to answer all my questions. In the second week of intense asana practice and fasting, my body began to shake during sun salutations, and I would stop immediately, totally confused. No one seemed to understand what was happening. One day, I moved into a position with arms extended above my head, head back, and heart open. Everything, the world as I knew it, stopped. "I" ceased to exist.

Breath and heartbeat stopped, and existence and nonexistence were the same pulsing light.

Cheryl believes she was only in this state a few seconds because she realized that, if she continued with such intensity, her nervous system would be damaged. So she relaxed the practice. In the nights that followed, she had difficulty sleeping and felt like a million volts of energy had been pumping through her body. Neither her teacher nor anyone at the retreat had an explanation for her.

Cheryl had plunged into this yoga experience with very little background and found herself in a community ill-equipped to support her. In similar situations, some students have told me they became disoriented and ended up lost and wandering the streets. A friend told me that, during her own transformative awakening experience in Asia, what supported her most was a good friend who made sure she had food and rest. After months in an Indian ashram, another friend nearly died of a stomach disorder until a doctor insisted she return to the US. Many people become seriously ill because of the food in these settings, and other environmental factors can make us very open and highly sensitive to extreme altered states. If a teacher, practice, or foreign setting is calling you, but you are unfamiliar with them, I suggest you do detailed research, speak to others who have been there, and if possible go with a friend or person you trust. Begin any practices gradually and establish a support system.

Qigong

Even though spiritual applications of qigong are currently out of vogue in China, this ancient art holds tremendous potential for spiritual awakening. It has been part of Chinese medical science and Taoist practices for more than 7,000 years.[27] Many Buddhist and Taoist masters recognize its transformative and healing gifts.

As the classic Chinese text, *The Secret of the Golden Flower*, states, "The celestial mind is like a house; the light is the master of the house. Therefore once you turn the light around, the energies throughout the body all rise. Just turn the light around. That is the unexcelled sublime truth."[28] Most of us find our inner light of awareness is preoccupied, even mesmerized by the outer circumstances of life and the corresponding thoughts and feelings these generate. This awareness shines from our eyes, enlivens our senses, witnesses our thoughts and emotions, and engages us in the world. By turning this light inward, letting go of the distractions of thought, and merging attention with our most subtle breath, we can know our true source. The "golden flower" of consciousness can awaken and unfold, penetrating and transforming our ordinary mind.

Taoist psychology distinguishes between our "original spirit" and a "conscious spirit." As Thomas Cleary points out, "The conscious spirit is historically conditioned, the original spirit is primal and universal. The conscious spirit is a complex of modifications of awareness, while the original spirit is the essence of awareness."[29] All our conditioned patterns, identifications, and unconscious parts of mind are part of the conscious spirit. The original spirit is pure consciousness, free of all conditioning and eternal by nature. It is considered the source of intuition, creativity, and inspiration.

Taoists understand that when original spirit awakens, the energies of our life force arise. So they physically circulate energy through the subtle body, with movements and the breath, in ways that accompany the turning inward of attention. Such practices balance awakening energies while increasing health and stamina in the body and clarity of mind. They include qigong practices such as the "microcosmic orbit," in which life-force energy, known as *qi* or *chi*, is circulated up the back and down the front of the spine. Some have used practices that reverse this orbit to sublimate and reverse the flow of sexual energy, so that it is converted into a powerful energy that enters the brain.[30]

When we practice qigong, we become aware of the power of life-force energy. As we learn to expand and circulate this subtle energy consciously, we may slip into an awakening. Even inexperienced practitioners may face issues similar to a kundalini awakening by circulating energy in qigong, as Becky experienced.

My first conscious experience with feeling the chi energy was when I took a class on seated qigong meditation, in which we concentrated on circulating the qi in an orbit in the body while listening to a tape of a Chinese master say the points in Chinese. I felt a lot of emotional energy, I wanted to burst into tears, but controlled it. A few days later, I was at home and my body began to jerk. I felt energy going up my arm, and vibrations in my arms and legs, followed by electrical sparks in my toes, my feet, and the crown of my head. During one meditation, I felt the energy going deeply into my lower back. I felt a jerk and a sensation going up my back from my waist to my neck. My back straightened involuntarily from the movement. Later, my fingers and hands became numb. I went to the doctor, but there was nothing medically wrong. I met with my qigong instructor and he told me that I was experiencing something psychological. He told me my meditation was not good because I was not smiling as I was supposed to, but it was very difficult to do with the energy surging and my body jerking. So my experience was not explained, nor was it validated. It became stressful to me, as I knew it was not merely psychological. I knew it related to qi energy, but it felt very strong and uncomfortable.

Becky's symptoms intensified when she attended a spiritual class, read a spiritual book, or had any new insight. She found that physical therapy helped her physical symptoms, and acupressure helped her relax and let go into the unfolding process.

Breathing Practices

Our breath is intimately related to prana, energy flow in the body. Breath is our connection with the universe and all that is in it. *Pranayama* practices are used in yoga to balance and harmonize breathing. By managing the movement of breath in the subtle body, kundalini energy can be safely activated and consciously directed. Yogis believe breathing exercises help us overcome obstacles and disease, increase longevity, and calm the mind for concentration and meditation. Yogis learn to invite more energy into the body by opening specific "locks," called *bandhas*, which also helps avoid some of the pitfalls of doing pranayama. The length and intensity of breathing practices are strictly monitored, as practitioners are introduced to them gradually. Many who do yoga today have learned alternate-nostril breathing, a beginning practice designed to bring the flow of breath in balance between *ida* and *pingala*, the two nadis on either side of sushumna in the center of the spine.

When done correctly, pranayama is very supportive of spiritual awakening. But according to classical teachings, those who do these practices overzealously can bring on difficulties such as perspiration, trembling, blackouts, hallucinations, blood-shot eyes, excessive heat in the body, and bleeding gums. If these are happening to you, give up the practices.

According to Pancham Singh, "Pranayama is nothing but a properly regulated form of the otherwise irregular and hurried flow of air, without using much force or undue restraint, and if this is accomplished by patiently keeping the flow slow and steady, there can be no danger."[31] He indicates that any impatience for yogic powers can cause problems for practitioners by putting too much pressure on the organs. This can cause pains in the ears, eyes, and chest, and digestive issues.

The *Gheranda Samhita* is a classical guide to practice that discusses factors influencing the effectiveness and safety of pranayama practice. These include an optimal environment, timing practice consistently and correctly, eating moderately, and purifying the nadis through cleansing practices. It recommends eating pure, sweet, cooling food to fill half the stomach, and avoiding bitter, acid, salt, pungent, and roasted things, wine, onions, berries, and many other items. It advises against food that is not easily digested, or hot, stale, very cooling, or very exciting. It also recommends that the yogi avoid much traveling, intimacy with women, warming by the fire, morning baths, fasting, and anything giving pain to the body.[32]

While this advice was passed down from another time and culture that offered living conditions we know little about, it suggests reasons for some of the difficulties Westerners may find doing practices like pranayama. Arousing kundalini was once done within guidelines for preparation and calm energy management. Today, many yoga practices are found on the Internet and in books. If we do them without good understanding, a supportive diet, or the right amount of effort, we risk creating too much energy charge, too fast, or disrupting our physical system. Some of the mysterious physical issues brought to therapists and doctors by practitioners may be related to this lack of preparation.

Transmission

Have you ever noticed that if someone starts laughing or coughing or telling a sad story in a room there is a resonance? Soon you are laughing, coughing, or feeling sad. In a similar way, the energies and consciousness of someone who is awakened can resonate with us if we are in their presence, available and open. This is transmission. Transmission is not magical. It works with how our energy fields communicate and resonate with one another.

Many of us feel drawn to spiritual teachers or gurus because, when we are in their presences, we feel transmissions through eye contact, touch, a meeting of minds, uniting in a stream of consciousness. They can convey a stillness or peace that draws students into trance-like states or into feeling deep meditative calm. This can all happen in person, on videos, or even through audio programs. Jonathan experienced a profound and unexpected shift in consciousness while traveling in India. He stumbled into the midst of a group led by an awakened mystic.

> In his presence, I felt a deep and mysterious resonance of an all-encompassing and nonpersonal love. Since that time, a blessed and choiceless devotion to the wordless mystery and the incredible challenges of embodiment has risen.

The ability to transmit energies does not necessarily mean the teacher is enlightened, as there are yogic techniques for developing the subtle body energy to impact other people. In fact, anyone with heightened energy has a potential of activating it within someone else, and some of us experience intense energetic or psychic responses to a lover, friend, or stranger. It may not be deliberate: the sender may be unaware but the receiver feels a strong impact. My body reacts when I am with someone who has active kundalini energy.

In Dzogchen, an advanced Buddhist path to liberation, the way to realization is found through transmission and a state known as *rigpa*, the state of naked awareness devoid of ignorance and dualism.

In ancient yoga lineages, the transmission of spiritual awakening was a rare gift to a devoted student who had already reached spiritual maturity. More commonly today, a guru offers *shaktipat* to awaken spiritual energy in the receiver. *Diksha* is another term for deliberately transmitting energy from one person to another with touch or eye contact. These transmissions may cause shifts in consciousness, trigger energetic responses, and possibly awaken kundalini. Swami Tirtha described it this way: "[Kundalini] is awakened by the favor of spiritual masters who by a mere touch or a kindly look do in a second arouse the kundalini shakti of those whom they are pleased to favor. This process is known as initiation through shaktipat, that is, transmission of Shakti."[33] Because the student usually lived in an ashram, there was ample support for whatever phases of spiritual awakening followed the initiation. Today very few teachers offer students the support and guidance that would draw them into an optimal and efficient conclusion to this process. People are left to their own devices and are usually without any clarity about their experience.

Transmission can be experienced as an energy entering the body, often through the third eye (ajna chakra), and some people respond to it by falling to their knees and bending backward, where they may stay motionless for a while in trance. It may not seem to have an immediate impact, but we feel energy activate later. And transmission can seem to have no impact at all. Swami Muktananda offered transmission to thousands of students in the 1960s, often by bopping students on the head with a peacock feather. Students who lived in his ashram reported that the energy was incredible. But despite the transmission, it does not seem that many ended up enlightened. They often felt a great impact, but spent many more years seeking to ground and live with spiritual insights. Many entered a kundalini process. Some are now in guru roles themselves, and others still struggle with somatic, psychological, and hallucinatory challenges.

Several clients of mine have attended a program in India called Oneness University, where they received transmission and then headed home to offer diksha to others. It sounds simple, but as energy shifts for these seekers they still need to work through unconscious material and learn to live with the phenomena of kundalini arising. Those who pass this transmission forward may have unresolved issues that block them from being clear channels for awakened energy, which may impact others adversely.

Dave traveled to Oneness University twice for several weeks of meditation and received diksha from the teachers. He was fortunate to be spiritually prepared and experienced. On the last day of the retreat, his group was declared awakened. They looked at each other in surprise because they felt no different. But during the months that followed, Dave felt a realization unfold.

I find uncanny synchronicity in my activity. I always seem to be, or end up, at the right place at the right time. The more I let go of my mind's tendency to make things happen or to be in control, the more I experience a flow and ease of living within this flow. Life is much more effortless and joyful. I get enjoyment out of doing the simplest things, like washing my face or tying my shoes. These are things that I would take for granted before while my mind was consumed about other things. I am the same "person" I always was, except that I now have more clarity and am not bothered by any mind chatter. Thoughts still happen and memory is easily accessed, but I no longer dwell on these. It's as if the background has become the foreground and the foreground has become the background. Awakening is not an end point, it is the beginning of a never-ending journey going nowhere! We are only uncovering what has always been here.

Many fully awakened people will describe the ordinariness Dave does. Transmission can be helpful for spiritual seekers, but it often requires a long period of spiritual maturing first. After transmission, we are not likely to wake up immediately though we may experience temporary feelings of blissful union. The work of deconstructing old patterns and energizing new ones can continue for years. Transmission can also be so subtle that there is no immediate response. Rather it gradually unravels old ways of being, so it's hard to say years later whether or not the transmission was really a trigger for awakening. Ultimately, all of us transmit who we are in every interaction. So it is not so surprising that someone who is resting in deep inner peace and wisdom can open the possibility of awakening in us.

Psychology

Teachers of awakening methods aren't equipped to handle everything that arises in students—whether it is anomalous events, spiritual awakenings, or energetic phenomena—so those who are awakening often turn to health professionals for support. However, modern psychotherapy has evolved toward behavioral approaches and using allopathic medicines to change inner experience. There are few therapists who are open to, and respectful of, the full range of human consciousness. As a result, we can harmfully contract our process rather than appreciate our insight and allow a natural unfolding. Experiences are often met with skepticism rather than open curiosity and support in both spiritual and therapeutic settings.

Therapists are generally so deeply trained in a black-and-white paradigm of "normalcy" and "illness" that there is very little room for the anomalous experiences that can occur with spiritual awakening. Although not all anomalies are spiritual, most spiritual experiences are outside the paradigm of normalcy. Thousands of people would benefit if we were to integrate alternate perspectives for viewing these events that did not pathologize the experiencer, nor try to block future experiences. Some psychological systems, such as Jungian analytical psychology, Holotropic Breathwork, psychosynthesis, Hakomi Method, and iRest Yoga Nidra do include practitioners who recognize the spiritual potential in shifts of consciousness.

Body Therapies

In the early 1900s, body therapies were introduced by Wilhelm Reich. Reich was a Freudian analyst who began to notice the limitations of talk therapy and started experimenting with breathing practices to release emotional blocks and facilitate the integration of insight. Because of the deep breathing these practices incorporate, energy often awakens following treatments. Reich called the energy field *orgone*, and to him a successful treatment caused a person to be fully orgasmic. Today this type of work is usually called bioenergetics or neo-Reichian therapy.

In the 1960s, psychiatrist Stanislof Grof sought to open people to transpersonal experience by deliberately activating energy releases. He called his process Holotropic Breathwork, and a session is done in groups with loud music in the background. Partners monitor and support the experience for each other. The work can involve reliving the trauma of birthing, and it can lead to many ecstatic and expansive spiritual moments. Gay Hendricks developed a similar program that is provided more individually, called Radiance Breathwork. Other forms of breathing practices came out of the rebirthing movement, including the primal scream fad. All of these practices deeply invigorate and alter breathing, while bringing up unconscious material and intense emotion.

About 20 percent of the people who contact me for help with energetic awakenings have been involved, at some time, in one of these movements. In the Age of Aquarius, people learned to let go of inhibition, at least temporarily, to breathe or pant, yell and scream, and generally release tensions held in their bodies. While very different from the classical breathing practices taught in yoga and tantra, these practices definitely open the body and sometimes trigger experiences of transcendence, visions, apparent past-life memories, heart-openings, and an interior sense of freedom. Here is a description of the energy awakening I experienced shortly after my first session working with Radiance Breathwork. I had fifteen years of meditation experience and five years of Jungian analysis by this time.

> I was sitting in a classroom, when a ball of energy suddenly began moving up from the base of my spine and into my head. It began slowly and then began to repeat in a fast and rhythmic way, rolling up over and over. With each roll, I began to feel higher and higher. My body became ecstatic, my mind fuzzy but open. I went into a little meditation room at the school and let go of anything else, letting the energy take me over. I fell into a sense of being unbound and my consciousness seemed to merge with space. After some time, the energy stopped rolling and I returned to a feeling of being present, open, and grounded. For nearly three months afterward, I could feel the bliss of this energy at will, and my sense of separation was gone. I could do any tasks that were needed, and knew who I was, but it was like looking at the world and the people in it with no sense of judgment or evaluation, just seeing their beauty and movements, and feeling no resistance to anything that happened.

Gradually I was pulled back into the ordinary challenges of work, graduate school, and family. I began to use breathwork more deliberately to address psychological issues. My personal experience was optimal for me, and raised no fear partly because of the supportive environment I was in at the time, and also because it was mostly blissful. Having a therapist and working with others who were familiar with this process meant I never had to feel it was a mistake or that I was verging on mental illness. My responsibilities and family kept me grounded in ordinary life.

Many who do breathwork or energy work have more difficult and overwhelming experiences, especially if extreme reactions were unanticipated and misunderstood. I saw a woman become catatonic for several days after an intense Holotropic Breathwork session. Once the energy is opened, it can continue to shake a person up for years.

Reiki, a more gentle and subtle hands-on healing method, has become quite a common practice, whether used for healing or as part of massages. Brenda was twenty-five when she first had an opening of energy during a Reiki session.

> The trigger happened at a Reiki healing night. I felt a rush of energy go up my back and shoot out of my head. I got hot, then freezing, energy, and burst out crying. It felt like a trip.

I have heard from many people who felt an awakening following a Reiki session. The sudden shifts in core energy can be alarming. Reiki, and other programs like Healing Touch and acupressure, are all designed to open different energy channels in the body—channels their founder once discovered can improve health and stimulate healing. Even so, it does not take much for life-force energy to be triggered, intensify, and move upward to stimulate an awakening.

"Substances" and Entheogens

Anthropologists found that plants with psychoactive elements have been used in many indigenous cultures during ceremonies and rituals to stimulate visions. Some researchers believe that the shifts in consciousness psychedelics produced contributed significantly to the evolution of indigenous cultures. Whether used by priests, shamans, or an entire community, insights from psychedelics may have factored into the development of societies.

A modern spiritual portal opened in the 1960s with LSD. Many of my colleagues, friends, and clients had their first introductions to expanded consciousness through it, which led them to seek similar experiences through spiritual practices. In the past few decades, more and more people have used plant medicines independently, with guides, or by participating in shamanic ceremonies. There are even a few approved churches dedicated to using consciousness-altering drinks made of psychoactive plants as part of their rituals. European laboratories have investigated the plant components and synthesized new mind-altering substances that have been used by thousands of people seeking highs, revelations, adventures in consciousness, and openings of mind and heart.

People often ingest these plants as an *entheogen*, which means "generating the divine within" and refers to using psychoactive substances to induce spiritual awakening. These substances include manufactured drugs like LSD and MDMA, and plant substances ranging from marijuana to mushrooms to ayahuasca, along with other natural plants that contain the psychoactive molecule 5-MeO-DMT, among other elements.[34] Those who use entheogens say they are nonaddictive and cause far fewer problems and deaths than alcohol use. In fact, it is exceedingly rare for anyone to die from an entheogen. All the same, they are considered a Class 1 substance in the US, too dangerous to be legal. The result is that few of these compounds and molecules have been adequately researched in the US because of legal risk.

People are drawn to travel in countries where these substances are used in ceremonial ways to alter consciousness and evoke spiritual, psychological, and physical healing. They often return needing some psychological support to deal with the energies and unconscious material that have arisen, and to ground themselves once again in the ordinary world. Despite some benefits, these substances can produce major distortions, triggering psychological confusion, anxiety, and occasionally long-term mental instability.

Michael began smoking marijuana in college and it made him feel euphoric, energized, and creative. When he started using psychedelic mushrooms, intense kundalini experiences arose along with overwhelming thoughts that caused him to panic.

Although my early experience with shrooms was very serene (I just felt calm, no thoughts, and at peace), one time I could feel this energy flowing up my spine and shooting out of my head. I felt wonderful for a few minutes. Then I started losing my mind. I remember exclaiming that I was a god. I felt euphoric. After a few moments, it started to terrify me. It was a huge shift in perspective and I didn't want to believe it. I remember thinking, "I like myself. I don't want to lose me."

Michael became overwhelmed by his thoughts, believing he might jump out of a window and kill himself. He was terrified and then he passed out. A friend helped him wake up but he was still flooded with thoughts.

I believed every single thought. I believed everything anyone told me. It was like every sound I heard was pure truth and I should believe it. For a week after, I didn't smoke or do anything but go to class. I was very happy and content, but I could feel the clarity that I had attained slowly slip away. I wanted it back and I thought that if I smoked again, it would return. Unfortunately, that's when things went really bad. I was back in my friend's apartment when it happened. I started panicking again as these ridiculous thoughts returned. It felt like electricity was flowing through everything and it was too much for me to handle. I passed out again and when I woke up, I completely lost myself. It took a while to remember that I had a mom and a dad and a family that I would see the next day.

Michael reported that, since this incident, he has felt always on the verge of panic. The energy activation and stimulation of the area in the brain known to produce hallucinatory experiences cause some psychedelic explorers to have a difficult time recovering.

Psychedelics can stimulate unconscious upheaval and temporarily induce mental distortions and fearful hallucinations. If this leads to a psychiatric hospitalization, and we are told we have a mental illness, the emotional scars can run deep, inhibiting spiritual seeking for many years. If we are given psychoactive medications to block or shut down an experience, we may also have to deal with difficult side-effects that block our capacity for good functioning and further spiritual growth.

It is unlikely any substance can create a permanent and deep sense of knowing the truth of who we are. We can enter an altered state that dramatically shifts our worldview, but the experience lacks the clarity essential for realization. Experiences move so quickly and erratically that the conscious mind is unable to process them. This can overcharge the energy field, causing weeks of turmoil. In some cases, our nervous system is disturbed and our sense of personal self is shaken without any awakening insights. As the neuroscientist Oliver Sacks said, "While it is understandable that one might attribute value, ground beliefs, or construct narratives from them, hallucinations cannot provide evidence for the existence of any metaphysical beings or place. They provide evidence only of the brain's power to create them."[35]

Unlike a meditation experience that can be ended at will, taking a pill or inhaling smoke cannot be undone until the physical process has played out. There is no predicting what will happen. Often people are in a foreign setting with teachers and companions they do not know while opening themselves up to complete release of control. Intention and personal history are major factors, and consequences can unravel for months and even years.

I advise anyone having difficulties with kundalini energy or invasive images and thoughts to avoid all intoxicants and mind-altering substances. Whenever overactivated, we need to direct attention to simply grounding ourselves by being in nature, eating healthy, and having quiet time. A sign of stable spiritual awakening is the ability to live in the moment with what *is* rather than grasping for the next big experience.

Shamanic Initiations

Shamanic practices bring awareness into other dimensions of consciousness that shamans call lower and upper worlds. Students take journeys into these dimensions and encounter animals, elements, landscapes, spiritual entities, and other powerful images. These worlds can be both shocking and healing as they open the psyche to inexplicable shifts even after journeys are finished. It is considered a gift to have psychic connections with other dimensions. Shamanic journeys most often occur while lying down and listening to rhythmic drumming. Sometimes they are facilitated by psychoactive plant substances. People doing these practices need solid, experienced guidance and a fearless perspective to expand into spirit and bring forward latent healing abilities.

Joyce is a client who kept frightening shamanic experiences to herself for years. When she tried to describe them to her closest woman friend, also a shamanic practitioner, the woman responded by saying she was possessed by an evil spirit and cutting off all communication. Fear-based interpretations of non-ordinary experiences are very damaging, and can take years to overcome. Another client, Veronica, described the aftermath of her shamanic journey this way:

> I started to experience huge rushes of energy after a head injury when I fell out of bed. No one could find a way to stop it and so I began searching for help. I found a shamanic therapist who did work with ayahuasca. This experience was intensely physical for me. Massive amounts of energy coming through me, like lightning bolts. I became frustrated and found it very difficult, but the therapist helped me to eventually let go, surrender, and eventually I felt my heart fill up with so much love I thought it was going to burst. I saw archetypes of a cobra and a goddess. It was beautiful. But I am still struggling with intense energy.

The responses and outcomes to shamanic journeys vary from one person to another, but they depend greatly on the wisdom of a guide. From a shamanic perspective, spiritual crises and even mental illness can signify the birth of a healer. Malidoma Patrice Somé, PhD, a shaman from the Dagara tribe in West Africa, argues that "Mental disorder, behavioral disorder of all kinds, signal the fact that two obviously incompatible energies have merged into the same field." He believes disturbances result when we don't receive assistance dealing with the presence of the energy from the spirit realm. To the Dagara, anyone going through a spiritual crisis has been chosen as a medium for a message to the community that needs to be communicated. When Somé came to the US, he was shocked to find people treated in mental institutions who he believed were having spiritual awakenings. He thought, "What a loss that a person who is finally being aligned with a power from the other world is just being wasted."[36] Indigenous perspectives of awakening can be valuable to us as we explore how to work effectively with psychic events, but we know very little about them. Some transpersonal therapists are trying to remedy this.

Spontaneous Moments

There are spontaneous portals to awakening not dependent on traditions or practices. Ready or not, we are suddenly plunged into a new consciousness and expression in the world. These are moments when we are completely present with what is happening and all mental clutter drops away. When energy and consciousness spontaneously move, spiritual awakening can be triggered by something completely unrelated to spiritual practice. Here are some triggers I have heard stories about.

Transformative dreams

Following periods of intense stress, despair, or grief

Feeling strong love or devotion

During or after sexual encounters

While reading books about awakening

As a result of falling off horses and hitting tailbones

After sitting with loved ones who are dying

As a result of food poisoning

While walking home from school

During or following childbirth

While witnessing beautiful sunsets

During and after surgeries

After deep therapy sessions

Following muggings

In the midst of severe emotional conflict or overwhelm

When spending many hours at a biofeedback machine

Doing visualization practices found on a website

During dying processes

Since energy and consciousness are interrelated, if one should awaken in us, the other is likely to follow soon. George would awake from dreams with his energy racing. During one afternoon nap, he heard an inner voice advising him to let go, followed by a spontaneous opening of awareness and energy.

> I had a vision of my whole life. A voice showed me that my life had been perfect, there was nothing else I could have done. There was no need for shame, regret, or guilt—I could let it all go. Then a flood of energy moved down to the base of my spine. I was super energetic for the next week and slept only four hours per night, but I felt great.

Sudden openings and revelations like George's can occur and then fall away as we return to the ordinary preoccupations of life with a new vantage point. They can also persist and push us more deeply into a spiritual process. They are a glimpse of truth or a moment of grace.

Dying

Images of death and fears of dying often arise as awakening progresses. Unfamiliar experiences arise that can make us feel like a part of us is dying, especially when our mind feels threatened as we release its control. Many Eastern scriptures describe awakening as an ego death. These thoughts and sensations are not about physical death, they are about internal clearing that lays the groundwork for new expressions of consciousness. This is how Mark described a moment of ego death.

> I was getting a massage when I started feeling like I was choking. Then I felt like I just completely disappeared, like I had died or something. I was just a white light in infinite black space. Since then, I've been thinking about death a lot, with a sense that I have died while alive—that my personality died.

While Mark was engaging a symbolic process of dying, the dying process itself also deeply touches us. Whether we have a near-death experience (NDE) or sit through the long hours with someone who is transitioning into death, we move out of the personal and into the universal. Encountering death moves us out of separateness and into unity.

After returning from an NDE, people report experiences of light, visions, new understandings of the unity of everything, and major energetic changes in their bodies. They enter a spiritual awakening process and feel blessed with the understanding granted to them. They may also be overwhelmed by disorientation, energy phenomena, and upheaval in the unconscious that is common during spiritual awakening. One woman described her NDE as traumatic because she kept hearing the words "You do not exist!" She struggled with this ego-dystonic message, as she was afraid of it. In an NDE, while the dying process is initiated, it is not completed, so many are drawn to spiritual awakening when they return. Kundalini energy may have risen in order to exit the body, which brings energetic and emotional consequences. While there may be trauma and physical damage to heal from, it is essential not to suppress any spiritual insight and understanding that has arisen, as it can offer vital direction in life. The insights gained during an NDE can be suppressed by medications or can turn a person into a celebrity. Neither situation is useful for spiritual growth, particularly if ego reasserts itself and identifies with a story.

When hospice workers, close family members, and loved ones with open minds and hearts are with someone transitioning into death, they can merge with the expansive consciousness present and experience part of the dying journey themselves. I believe a form of transmission can occur that triggers awakening. Sensing the vastness of death nearby can feel like an out-of-body experience. Some people tell me about later visitations from the one who passed. Others report kundalini energy arising. Awareness can be more fluid, inclusive, and tuned in to being one with everything. Also, intense grief can open us to an awakening or trigger spiritual seeking.

In a wonderful book called *The Grace in Dying*, a Buddhist psychologist and hospice worker teaches that if we do not awaken during our lifetime, there is a final chance to do it as we prepare to die.

> We are, in fact, returning to our original state as everything dissolves. Body and mind are unraveled, as are the connections from one level of manifestation to another, including those connections of the energy field with the nervous system and those connections that anchor the life force on the physical plane. As these die so too do the emotions, the desires, the dualisms, all previous structures of identity— and there is a gap. This gap is all openness, a sense of bodily solidity dissolving.[37]

In Tibetan Buddhism, this gap is referred to as a *bardo*. Eastern spiritual practices for the dying are designed to help release attachments, just as spiritual awakening releases them. Letting go of attachments and ego orientation often feels like dying, as we realize the insubstantiality and illusory nature of our thoughts, beliefs, and emotions.

Trauma

Over the years, I have met people who were thrust into spiritual emergence through an act of violence. One woman, a long-term yoga practitioner, was mugged. It resulted in shifts of energy, involuntary shaking, altered consciousness, and a vast openness that lasted for months. Patrick experienced a series of traumatic shocks when he was twenty years old: he was beaten unconscious by three gang members, caused a serious car crash that left him hospitalized, suffered emotional problems after his girlfriend left him for his best friend, and was erroneously placed on academic warning. Not a spiritual seeker at the time, he was completely unprepared for what happened.

> *I had just finished watching a World Series baseball game with my father and was walking down the hall to what had been my childhood bedroom. Without warning, it was as though I was struck by lightning. I dropped to the floor and started shaking violently. I felt energy gathering and rising from deep inside me. It pushed upward through my heart and throat. I had previously been feeling very heavy and dense. As the energy roughly pushed its way through, that feeling got lighter and thinner. I experienced a vast emptiness. The feeling of what I thought was "me" was disappearing. There was no thinking. It was not possible. There was just the experience of energy and sensation giving way to nothing. At the point where it seemed I would disappear completely, whatever remained of "me" tried very forcefully to hang on. I torqued my torso, clenched and tightened*

*arms and legs—all of which caused great pain. It seemed I had
a choice between pain and nothing. I chose pain. Some of the
blockages and physical issues I'm dealing with today at age
sixty-five appear to be related to that choice.*

Patrick recovered from these traumas to have a successful and
interesting life. But during retirement his presence at the drowning
death of a family member triggered the anxiety suppressed in his
body. He had renewed energy releases, physical pain, and serious
insomnia. His solution has been to work with his body using iRest
Yoga Nidra meditation, a gentle release system developed to treat
post-traumatic stress disorder (PTSD).[38]

Many people suffer from PTSD after sexual or physical abuse,
street violence, war, and displacement from family and home. The
psychological and energetic blocks that result can last indefinitely.
We become more physically contracted and prone to illness, anxiety,
defensiveness, and self-protection. Our spirit can be demoralized,
which keeps us from living our full potential. Shamans have called
this a loss of soul. In some cases, physical shock opens life-force
energy, especially if it affects the base chakra where kundalini is
coiled or if it involves an NDE. Some people leave their bodies and
observe an attack from a distance. Brain damage may result in a
changed perspective or an openness to visions and light. We can
begin a habit of detaching from our body under stress, which therapists call *dissociation*. And medical treatment may change our body
chemistry and produce other unfamiliar sensations and mental
shifts such as visions, brain fog, and insomnia. Any of these things
can make trauma into a portal as energy gets activated and consciousness discovers that it is not limited to form. This can change
our worldview.

Sexuality

Yogic scriptures say sex can be a portal to awakening for household-
ers. During orgasm all identifications and attachments can fall away.

If we are able to stay aware in this emptiness so that it holds steady and expands, we can momentarily awaken. As described earlier, in some tantric traditions, sexual arousal is a method for awakening energy at the base of the spine and consciously bringing it upward so that, instead of a genital release, an entire body orgasm culminates in a shift of consciousness into expanded awareness. Yogis warn that this is a risky method, as it can cause a person to become addicted to sex and dependent on a partner.

Life-force energy can arise in a sexual relationship, whether through intensity of love, concentrating on sensation, or because one partner transmits active kundalini to the other. If this other person is not aware of kundalini and has no spiritual context, then its rising can be disconcerting. If the energy stays active and becomes uncomfortable, the person may feel his or her partner has done something that is unwanted, even dangerous.

Caroline was a forty-year-old psychologist who felt kundalini awaken after a long day of lovemaking with a man she felt was her soulmate.

We were sleeping in a vacation home on a small island when my lover awakened with a dream of small entities who were outside the house wanting to come in. As they broke into the house he ran to the door (in the dream) to slam it and as he did the actual door in the bedroom slammed shut and woke both of us. As he told me the dream I became frightened. Then the knob on the door suddenly turned and opened and light poured through. Suddenly all my energy was thrown down to the base of my spine and then built upward. As the energy arose my body arched back. Deep breathing patterns took over, came all the way up and over my head and through my mouth, and I screamed an incredibly loud and piercing sound. When the sound stopped the door slammed shut. During this experience, my lover saw light energy forms spinning around in a whirl, followed by an enormous eagle that swept over our heads. After the door shut, the space was clear and very still. We began to repeat a mantra used to invoke the power of light until light came through the skylight above us in the morning.

While unanticipated openings, especially strange psychic events like what Caroline describes, can shock body and mind, when we stay grounded with them we can integrate and reap the benefits. Sexual awakening is a great initiator, but enlightenment is knowing connectedness with the whole of life from a deep interior place, and living from that knowing. Our encounters with others are transient and impermanent, no matter how impactful and loving.

Stress and Grief

Serious stress and anxiety can stir kundalini energy. It's as if the body takes in so much input that the nervous system explodes. For some this looks like a nervous breakdown, for others it's a sudden breakthrough into the vastness of something new and unknown. James was about to become a physician. He came from a very rigid family and was under extreme pressure because he was uncertain about his career choice, angry that his father insisted he became a doctor, exhausted by his studies, and about to take major exams.

> *One night, while looking into the bathroom mirror, I suddenly fell into an experience and realization of true forgiveness, and a huge surge of energy came through my body that made me feel ecstatic. Everything I had been carrying fell away as the energy flowed through me. My mind became quiet and clear. When I went to sleep that night, it was the most blissful sleep with colorful dreams. For the next few months, I felt one with the universe and free like the Buddha—even with the schoolwork I had to complete.*

For James, the pressure in the moment forced a breakthrough. For Carson, stress built over the course of twenty-two years led to divine surrender. After an abusive marriage, adopting two emotionally disabled children, having multiple injuries and illnesses including two NDEs, living through a house fire, and experiencing divorce and financial ruin, his awakening occurred while on an airplane flight.

> *When I surrendered my life to God, I was suddenly washed by a white light that cleansed me of all negative thoughts, feelings, and emotions. For the next five months, I experienced intense energetic and vibrational activity, changes in my body, intense bliss, love, oneness, intuition, energy, synchronicities, knowing and sense of Godliness. Then, for the past year and a half I've been in a dark night of the soul with profound depression, fear, anxiety, dissociation, cognitive dysfunction, loss of direction, absence of identity, and inability to work.*

Carson's experience includes the ups and downs many find so distressing in a process of awakening. A sudden burst of physical and psychic freedom brings such joy after a life of feeling burdened, and yet this wonderful experience does not endure. Carson needed to face residual feelings from his traumatic life, come to peace with shifts in identity, and find ways to work at a slower pace. This is how stress can be a portal into freedom. It may not feel like it: Who wants life to fall apart? Who welcomes challenges that overwhelm and cause pain? But when our world breaks, it also changes. We see life through a new lens. Grief works similarly. When we are able to break through grief, we discover new resources we never realized we had—including a peace and love that is greater than us. While grief feels like loss, it can be a powerful spiritual turning point.

Internet Awakenings

It seems anything we wish for can be found on the Internet, and practices for awakening are among them. This brings us more options to raise energy and shift consciousness, but it has many risks: teachers can be poorly qualified, they may never personally meet with students, and students have no way to evaluate their ability to help with challenges. The practices taught may not be optimal for students considering their mental states, lifestyles, understandings, and the possibility of latent psychiatric problems—which can all lead vulnerable students to breakdowns if energies become too intense.

Connie was hoping for answers to financial challenges and problems related with a breast surgery. She was happy and expectant when she found an online energy-healing class that she believed would help. Then she did an autohypnosis session.

> *Suddenly something very weird happened. I entered an altered state and felt a powerful vortex of indescribable energy pouring out of my head. I didn't understand what it was, so I wasn't scared; on the contrary I felt peace and thought that this was the energy that was supposed to heal me. The energy seemed to pull me further back into myself and I felt as if I was to dematerialize, so I mentally stopped it and opened my eyes. Afterward I was excited and unable to sleep, thinking about what happened and feeling the energy pouring out of my head and hands.*

While some of these programs effectively activate energy, they can rarely offer the depth of personal support needed to model awakened life and to navigate the challenges we tend to encounter along the way. If you find yourself overwhelmed after Internet practices, stop doing them and spend more time in nature, making art, or cooking. Find a friend or therapist who can help you reorient to your life before engaging more explorations.

Spontaneously Not-Knowing

Awakening ultimately drives us to encounter the unknown and not-knowing, which can happen at any time. The anonymous fourteenth-century writer of *The Cloud of Unknowing* and *The Book of Privy Counseling* taught that the contemplative way of knowing God arises by forgetting everything we know—giving up beliefs, studies, and ideas—to know God through love. He wrote that between God and human life is a great forgetting that we enter through contemplation. Similarly, all forms of meditation release attachment to thought and emphasize experiencing our essence, prior to thought, through love or silence. Hindu scriptures describe *sat*, the direct encounter with pure existence that is free from the delusions, images, and expectations of the separate self. When felt as consciousness, it is absolute silence, stillness, radiant expansion, or love and bliss. These are all states beyond mental knowing. They collapse our personal center of gravity as an identity and ego. What remains is simple, open, and available to navigating life with intuition and authentic movement. Life is lived moment to moment, meeting *what is* without resistance or clinging to expectations and beliefs.

This potential is available to anyone. It is a portal that opens spontaneously for unknown reasons, likely within conditions nurtured by earlier energetic, emotional, or meditative efforts. This portal can initiate a cleansing of old patterns and dynamics, and it can rearrange our subtle energies. We enter a spontaneous journey that is not controlled by will or intention, and we begin feeling out of control because we never know what to expect. The truth is, life has always been lived as a great unknown. But the illusion of a separate and unique self has kept our mind deluded into thinking it has both understanding and control. We long to predict what will happen and we consistently make choices based on these predictions, believing we have control over our destinies. But conditioning impacts those choices, and our predictions are often wrong. Awake consciousness is, and always has been, completely open to the unexpected. We can use glimpses into not-knowing to help us relax into this mystery, and to be at peace with the ways awakening changes our body and mind.

Anomalous Experiences

Sometimes we can be absorbed in an experience that is so full, and yet so unfamiliar, that it changes our perceptions about human possibilities. These anomalies do not fit any model accepted in mainstream culture. They are inexplicable and yet their power is undeniable.

Thousands of people who are sane, healthy, and engaged in productively mainstream lives sometimes encounter the fringe of human experience in psychic phenomena, UFO encounters, remote viewing, astral travel, channeling, past and future life memories, alternate universes, and infusions of archetypal energies.

I respect anomalous experiences as part of human potential. I believe that, when an event jolts consciousness out of ordinary boundaries, the way is paved for a deeper search. Anomalous portals make us curious about the range of human potential and reveal the fluidity of our awareness. Whether or not these events are "real" in the way that witnessing a tree or a sunset is real, they mysteriously occur. They can have a profoundly transformative effect on the direction of our life, for better or worse, depending on how they are interpreted. I'd like to discuss some of them in depth.

Past-Life Regression

When we tune in to a story from a previous life that has symbolic meaning in this life, past-life memories can be useful transpersonal experiences. I once participated in a subtle regression through guided hypnosis. In the first regression, I shivered in extreme cold and experienced myself as a young boy dying in a cold cave where I had been sent because of leprosy. The experience was intense and clear, and not completely out of the framework for this life. The regression brought up abandonment, an issue I addressed in therapy in this life after my mother died suddenly. It was powerful to work with that theme from a larger point of view. I became intrigued with past-life regression as a way to work with deep psychological patterns that are carried from life to life.

Another way past-life memories are a portal to awakening is when they help our current life come into focus. I felt this powerfully when during a regression I experienced myself as a young boy going through a long shamanic initiation. For months, there would be times when my body was filled with energy and I would run at night through open plains under a vast blanket of millions of stars. The sensation was breathtakingly beautiful and internally powerful—I could feel it in every cell of my body. Recalling this past life as a shaman was a life-altering event for me because it brought sensations I had not known in this life. I experienced moments when my mind was spacious, open, and free of thought. I also felt how I struggled to be a helpful guide to members of my tribe. Even the end of that life offers a message to me, when I encountered a tiger and willingly surrendered to it—and to death. Today, more than thirty years after doing this regression, I can see how it offers a vision of the work I have done for most of my career in this life. What I thought would be just an interesting experience profoundly impacted the roles I have carried ever since.

Channeling

A client named Patricia opened me to other-dimensional perspectives, and taught me to respect those who channel other beings or who feel influenced in a helpful way by encounters beyond the ordinary. The spirit within us has a vast potential that is mostly untapped, perhaps even inaccessible to most people. There is a great gift in being curious, rather than suppressive, when non-ordinary experiences like channeling arise.

Patricia lived on a ranch, cared for abandoned animals in her spare time, and was married to an airline pilot. She did not use any mind-altering substances, nor did she practice any meditation. In hypnosis one day, Patricia described herself as lying nearly unconscious in a sarcophagus in a great pyramid. She said she was a priestess and the daughter of a king in Sumer who had been sent for an initiation. Suddenly her voice changed. In a lovely, lyrical tone she told me her name was Aesthenia. She had joined with Patricia during this ancient life in Egypt, as Patricia's consciousness left her body in the pyramid, which enabled her to become a seer and guide. Aesthenia described herself as being from another dimension.

Over several months I met regularly with Patricia, and Aesthenia returned to tell her story, offer predictions about the future, and speak of the merging of beings like herself with humans to enrich consciousness on the earth plane. She said she had been with Patricia for five lifetimes. Patricia began to remember more and more of the sessions and gradually was able to connect with Aesthenia through meditation. Patricia became more psychic, developed an artistic ability, learned hands-on healing, grew interested in ancient history, and traveled to Egypt where she visited the pyramids. For a while she gave psychic readings to friends, but then saw that they were looking for answers from her that they could find within themselves, so she stopped. As Patricia's life unfolded, her inner wisdom and sense of peace grew. She eventually returned to a quiet life, enjoying her family, her animals, and her art.

I do not believe that pushing into other dimensions, or into channeling them, through workshops and evocations is especially useful to the awakening process. When they arise spontaneously, they can be a portal bringing gifts that support integration. Therapists need to be open to experiences like this. Channeling is meaningful, simply because it is meaningful to those experiencing it, and it can help us grow and awaken.

Visions

The literature of spirituality in every tradition includes revelations from divine beings, visitations from guides or deceased loved ones, images of gods and goddesses, and appearances of soaring eagles or snakes or other creatures—both real and mythological. Visions can be compensatory when certain areas of the brain are not functioning, including in times of deep withdrawal such as lengthy meditations or in isolation. They are produced in sleep and sometimes arise in waking states.[39] Many psychoactive drugs and plant medicines trigger visions because of the areas they target in the brain, and it seems likely that the energy of kundalini produces visions when it rises and penetrates those same brain receptors. We often encounter archetypal images in visions that represent aspects of the psyche that are arising to be recognized and integrated during a transformative process.

Caleb was facing life as a paraplegic after a devastating automobile accident. He described leaving his body and witnessing the accident, then waking up later in the hospital. For days he saw visions of Indian gods and goddesses hovering around his room, even though he had never studied Eastern religion or practices, and had no idea who they were. He felt completely disoriented as he faced his next step in life, but he had a newfound interest in spirituality.

Laurie was a practicing Buddhist in her thirties when she told me about some early visions she had, prior to a very difficult time of loss in her life.

At the age of sixteen, while visiting my family in Spain, I had a vision of Christ emerging from the armoire in front of my bed. Staring in disbelief at Christ, I sensed a glowing and warm sensation over my heart as Christ smiled into my eyes and reached his hand toward me. I felt enveloped with unconditional love. He was letting me know that everything would be okay.

The most common extrasensory experiences reported by people in a spiritual emergence process are occasionally hearing a voice with a message or seeing a symbol or vision. Often they happen before a major crisis or turning point in life, as if some loving source wants to offer support for what is to come. They may occur in meditation. They can also happen to a person who is not in a spiritual process, and they are not signs of psychosis. (I'll discuss the difference between visionary experiences and psychosis in chapter 6.) Visions of Christ or Mary are common archetypal images that arise in a spiritual awakening, and the descent of light or an internal experience of light has been part of mystical experience for centuries. Gabrielle was volunteering as a social work intern at a Native American reservation when she had this experience.

I was camping in a tipi, in the middle of the woods. I had to go to the bathroom but it was 4 a.m. and I was scared of bears. So I decided to just go right outside the tipi. Then a light, about the size of a flashlight, came toward me from the woods. The light started moving faster. It was moving faster than any human could ever run. It continued to come right toward me, but I didn't feel afraid. Instead, I felt curious. When it reached the edge of the trees before entering the clearing where I was, it shot up ten feet in the air and hovered for a second. Then it shot up another ten feet and hovered for a second. Then it shot up another ten feet till it cleared the trees and hovered in the sky for a few seconds longer and then shot off into the sky. The words, "Take care of your mother" came to me. I wondered what that meant and then went back to bed. In the morning I was told that my maternal grandmother had died the night before.

Some people would interpret this as a message from Gabrielle's grandmother, some would think of it as a UFO experience, and others would heed the strong psychic message she received. We can't know or understand why these kinds of anomalies occur, so while they are open to interpretation, what matters is how we experience their meaning personally.

Here is an initiatory vision described by Raymond. His vision expresses both the fearful depths and the potential for expansion that can occur along a spiritual process.

While meditating I began to breathe regularly without having to count my breaths, and my mind was clear. Then I started to have brief visions, like coming in and out of dreams. There was a circle of people standing in a kitchen. I was sitting on the floor in the middle of the circle. Everyone was tall and looking down at me, so I think I was a child. I sat there, holding a basket with a lid that had something inside, something bad, something dark. A woman told me that everyone was there to help and protect me from whatever was inside the basket. I was scared to open it, but I knew it had to be done. I removed the lid to reveal a bottomless pit, a dark abyss. The darkness came flying out of the basket and everything went black.

This kind of vision is like a waking dream that the mind produces, possibly to get our attention. There are many images in this experience that Raymond could work with, as if in a dream: a strong female figure, a supportive group, a dark abyss where the unconscious rests. By working with the elements of visions with a therapist who specializes in dreamwork, we can perceive their messages. We may develop a rich, meaningful, and even prophetic dream life when we are encouraged to pay attention to it. When we find the vivid images intriguing, rather than frightening, they can serve us well—even bringing portents of spiritual realization.

Shifts of Perspective

So many additional phenomena and anomalous moments arise within human awakening. Consciousness is very creative. These events may not be spiritual portals but they startle us out of complacency and have major impacts on our lives. They can make a spiritual seeker out of a realist or confirmed skeptic. I am referring to experiences such as levitation, out-of-body travel, seeing spaceships, meeting other-worldly or other-dimensional beings, feeling a continual interior light, perceiving energy fields or auras in people and places, psi phenomena like bending metals with the mind, hearing inner guides who appear in times of need, or seeing ghosts or spirits. Many who have lost loved ones feel their presences, talk with them, or see them in dreams. While not spiritual awakenings, these strange events raise questions and doubts that can initiate the journey of spiritual seeking.

As we engage the many portals of awakening, no matter which ones we encounter, know this: we are being invited to grow. Consciousness is ready for a new perspective. There may never be a completion to the process of awakening, just as there may never be an end to the potential of evolution. The universe and God are infinite. We live in a mystery beyond what the mind can conceive. All the same, we can relax into a quiet happiness and open acceptance of whatever each day brings.

Even so, internal changes triggered by the many spiritual portals we have discussed can create chaos in our mind as it clings to what is familiar and to limited, conventional ideas about sanity. Without understanding that we are being invited to embrace a new perspective, we might think:

"I want to be the way I was before."

"I feel so different from everyone else, even my longtime friends."

"I have no idea what to do, nothing I used to care about matters any longer."

These are some of the challenges we will explore in the next chapter.

PART TWO

NAVIGATING THE CHALLENGES OF AWAKENING

5. Challenges That May Come with the Process

Spiritual awakening may initially result in an ecstatic period of time when we feel clarity and openness to life, as it is. We may feel free from a troubling history or from painful patterns of thinking. We can feel absorbed in wonder or love. This is a period of grace. It is often followed by a time when unfamiliar and challenging conditions arise because having a period of deconstruction and reorientation is necessary to learning to live with awakened perspective. I will discuss how this works more in chapter 8.

The challenges of awakening we will look at in this chapter are understood to be part of the awakening process by cultures with long histories of cultivating it. Consider your own awakening events as you read this chapter. My hope is that you will find a description here to ease your mind, let you know that what you went through is important and valuable, and encourage you to reap its many benefits by accepting it. Should you encounter these challenges in the future, this chapter will prepare you to meet them with understanding. Viewing the awakening process this way is important because its challenges are not considered "normal" within Western religious and psychological perspectives. Culturally, we have demonized or pathologized many of them, as I will discuss in the next chapter. For now, read through these common challenges with an open mind and heart, knowing that alongside you many others have also encountered them.

Effects of Kundalini Energy Rising

Traditionally, students of yoga are given preparatory training to ease the effects of kundalini energy and awaken it through optimal channels. As a result, they experience fewer overwhelming events. Depending on the lineage, these methods include using asana to make the body open and limber, doing internal cleansing exercises, adhering to strict dietary requirements, gradually adding advanced breathing and meditation practices, practicing celibacy, and releasing ego tendencies through things like obedience to a teacher. Only when a student is ready are the specific breathing practices taught that gently bring kundalini up.

These days, most who activate this energy and report difficulties have not done much preparation—and are not interested in doing it. The result can feel chaotic. In extreme cases, the intensity of initial kundalini activation has been compared to a hurricane or massive explosion, feeling so powerful it could kill. For some, this is terrifying. For others, it leaves ecstasy and unitive consciousness in its wake. In her book *Biology of Kundalini*, Jana Dixon describes the experience as "a thousand volts of electricity" and "ten-thousand orgasms." She says it is "the most extreme experience one can endure energetically."[40]

Each experience with kundalini is unique and depends on personal history, belief system, personality, lifestyle, health, and many other factors. Emotionally charged traumas may be sustained anywhere in our body or spirit, and when those locations are energized, they release from the energy field. These traumatic memories can impact the way our awakening process unfolds. Here are some common phenomena that may accompany, or arise following, a kundalini awakening. These are usually temporary, and no one is likely to experience all of them.

Anxiety, even terror

Appetite changes and digestive issues

Changes in sexual desire

Ecstasy or blissful vibrations

Emotional swings

Energy rushes and, later, feeling blockages

Expanded consciousness

Fear about being ill or dying

Heat or burning sensations

Heart palpitations, discomfort, or chest expansion*

Hearing inner sounds

Insomnia or awakening long before sunrise

Involuntary movements

Night sweats

Out-of-body sensations or loss of self

Physical pain where energy from past trauma has been stored*

Rush of energy upward from feet, perineum, or solar plexus into the head

Spontaneous yoga postures or hand movements

Stirring at the base of the spine as energy releases

Vibration or shaking

One of the greatest surprises is when kundalini rising feels like a quantum jump out of what feels normal to us. We are leaping into a new way of being, which can feel as challenging as inspiring. These shifts may arise for months and even years. Do not panic! You are not going to die. Your energy will eventually become more calm and subtle. Be patient, accepting, and take time to adjust life to include new patterns. Chapter 7 will offer supportive ways to do this.

Releasing Energetic Blockages

We are engaging a process of clearing and transformation. Awakening is becoming integrated throughout our body-mind, so

---

* It is always advisable to get a medical examination if there is any persistent pain, discomfort, or symptoms of illness, as the energy may be amplifying a medical issue that was dormant before awakening.

for weeks, months, or years after an initial event, we need to address blockages so kundalini can flow. These blockages can be felt emotionally, sensed intuitively, or can manifest as physical pain. They may reveal a psychological or medical issue that needs to be addressed.

As discussed in chapter 2, when kundalini energy journeys upward, it moves through sushumna, located in the central channel of the spine. Schools of yoga identify three, sometimes four, major energetic blockages that it can encounter along the way. These knots, called *granthis,* correspond with points in our body that hold particularly strong attachments and identifications with desires and beliefs. As energy touches these knots, assumptions about our self and our lives are challenged. We are forced to face thoughts and emotions that are inauthentic or self-limiting, based on inadequate understanding of who we are. On a spiritual journey, we encounter these issues in order to move beyond them, so it is important to consider each one.

Solar Plexus Blockage

In the subtle body, the solar plexus is a significant energetic crossing point as we move out of identification with the physical body, through the lower chakras, and into the upper three chakras, which relate with spirit. The belly is where the struggle to be our true self seems to take place. It is where we feel attached to pleasure, material things, and having things go our way. It is where we address issues of will and power. Spiritual awakening challenges assumptions about our needs, whether for comfort, luxury, status, or affirmation. It crumbles our personal attachments while paradoxically demanding our authenticity. As we struggle with issues of identity and control, our bellies may churn or become knotted and hard. As we breathe in, we can direct our breath to the affected area. As we breathe out, we can practice letting go of attachment and identification. Physically, we may need to simplify our diet and reduce stress, in ways I discuss in chapter 7.

Heart Blockage

In the heart area, we feel attached to emotions, certain people, treasured beliefs, and objects of passion. We also hold childhood wounding in the heart, from times when we reached out and were rejected or felt disillusion, judgment, and loss. We created armoring to block vulnerability. To live an awakened life, we must open the constrictive ways we have responded to past hurts, and sometimes this happens spontaneously during intense suffering and grief. The heart seems to crack open and a heart-awakening occurs, flooding us with love. When the heart is open, we can enjoy life and engage the world authentically.

Most spiritual traditions have practices to open the heart. Whether through compassion, unconditional love, forgiveness, kind action, service, worship, or devotion, they recognize that energies of the heart serve the evolution of our spirit, and enhance the capacity for inner and outer peace. When our heart begins to open, we often recognize how we have blocked expressions of love, and we see the limitations of personal love because it tends to want reciprocity. As the heart expands, we begin to intuit the essence of universal, impersonal love.

We can experience slight pain, contraction, or burning sensations as the blockages release from the heart. It is important not to dismiss heart pain, racing heartrates, or irregular heartbeats, even when symptoms correlate with your awakening process. Check with your doctor first to see if it is something you need to heal with medical attention. Then work with practices from your own tradition, counselors who can help you process any grief or loss, or the gentle heart-opening practices taught in yoga and qigong systems. Do something nurturing each day that helps you express love for others, for the earth, and for yourself. Cultivate gratitude.

Third-Eye Blockage

Some meditation practices focus on the third eye, in the middle of our forehead, because yogis consider it a command center for the other chakras. With this chakra open, intuition helps us more easily manage all energetic activity, but non-ordinary experiences may increase. In deep meditation, this area may throb. We may develop headaches or stimulate buzzing, itching, and crawling sensations in the head. Phenomena attributed to opening the third eye include colors, intense light, visions of divine beings, insights, psychic abilities, automatic writing, dissolution of ego-identity, perceiving expansive unity, and forming a mind-to-mind link with a guru.

Psychic abilities are easy to attach to and make part of our personal identity. We can become distracted by feeling special or mistakenly think the powers indicate spiritual completion. In most traditions, psychic practices are considered obstacles to spiritual realization—to be ignored or avoided. Even so, some of my clients experience them as an essential area of growth. Information obtained through psychic means can bring insights into the nature of existence and personal issues. When psychic gifts are used neither to feed ego nor for commercial gain they can initiate a capacity to help heal and support others. I suggest using wise discrimination and getting solid advice before stepping into roles that depend on psychic abilities.

If you are uncomfortable with strong intuitions, frequent visitations, or are overwhelmed by any phenomena, work with a skilled psychic to learn more about setting boundaries. You can determine the intensity and frequency of your openness. This is essential, because third-eye openings sometimes include frightening images, voices that never seem to stop, and other distressing content that can lead to a spiritual emergency. It feels like an area of our brain becomes too open and will not shut off. Substances, shamanic practices, and traumatic childhood histories can contribute to this disorientation. Psychotherapy and medication may be temporarily beneficial to block invasive psychic experiences, especially if they are frequent or you are not sleeping well. A safe place to rest and deep therapeutic work also help.

Throat Blockage

Some yogic systems identify a granthi in the throat chakra. With a blockage here, you might experience energy arising and feel a contraction as it reaches the throat or struggle with speaking, swallowing, or a shaking head. Psychologically, the throat can be blocked due to habits of withholding our truth and not speaking up for our self. As children, many of us were not allowed to say anything that upset parents or schoolteachers, and trained ourselves to hold back feelings and opinions. Some of us took in spiritual ideas that convince us anger should never be expressed, and hold in justifiably angry feelings that need an outlet. Counseling can help these emotions move by talking about them or feeling them in a safe place. You might also use the *bij* mantras, described in chapter 7, which are yogic vibratory sounds that open the throat and allow energy to move upward. If physical problems persist, a medical or dental evaluation can investigate esophageal issues and jaw disorders, as these can also contribute.

Facing Our Psyche

Some spiritual seekers believe an awakening will erase all psychological issues, but this is not true. During an awakening we may feel completely free of history and personal identity. While some beliefs, preferences, or habits fall away or transform immediately, after the initial euphoria settles even deeper issues and patterns surface. For an awakening to stabilize, we must see through these patterns and attachments by recognizing them as illusions and memories of the separate self that are no longer relevant to life in this moment. Until we release the past, we feel divided in our allegiance and caught in the "I got it, I lost it" syndrome of falling in and out of awakened states.

We can feel changed after a beautiful revelation, and still there is unfinished business: parts of our suppressed psyche that need to be seen clearly and integrated. When we are more comfortable with our personal story and have reached more resolution for psychological distress, we are more prepared for the awakening process. Louisa is a Zen practitioner who was troubled by mood swings after a satori awakening.

> Free-floating, negative emotions would arise—such as fear, shame, anxiety, grief—without any content or story attached. Old emotions were being cleared out and there was no need for me to know what any of them were about. There have been intensely challenging recurring "dark night" phases, filled with discomfort and fear. At the same time, on another level, I feel interest, trust, and a lack of concern. All of this happens against a background of bliss.

Louisa describes a calm ability to observe her range of emotions without becoming entangled and alarmed. As we face our psyche, we too can see through aspects of ego, woundedness, and the separate self without feeling wrong for having experienced them. Through acceptance of our whole self, we eventually get past these challenging stages and feel more stable in our realization. Here are some of the things we can encounter within our psyche.

Anxiety about changes in self, relationships, or life

Depression or loss of "me"

Doubt that "someone like me" can awaken

Emotions and moods that feel sudden and irrational

Extreme energy followed by extreme tiredness

Fear of energy or shifts in consciousness

Inability to cope with toxic environments or people

Inability to tolerate crowds or overstimulation

Loss and self-blame after the bliss of a realization fades

Mental confusion and cloudy thinking

Overwhelming releases of love and compassion

Past trauma resurfacing through memories and feelings

Psychic reactivity to traumatic events in the world

Sensitivity due to astrological changes like full moons

Sleep terrors or erratic sleep patterns

Stories or déjà-vu moments remembered from previous lives

Uncertainty about life and death

Unexpected shifts in mood, often with no outward cause

After an awakening, life can feel like a rug pulled out from under us. It is natural to occasionally feel anger, guilt, fear, and sadness about the loss of the old "me." Counseling support can be important as we move into a new life. If we are so overcome by emotion that we cannot care for the basic needs of our human self, we will not move forward spiritually. The two go hand in hand. If it seems that your life is falling apart, address the issues surfacing before you reach for the next step of spiritual maturity. The spirit within us supports cultivating authentic and healthy lifestyles.

At some point in awakening, we see that we are not our thoughts and not our emotions. They are passing experiences collected from our history that entangle the energy field as it attempts to become clear, empty, and open to life. When we see this clearly, our true nature helps us step back into its presence so that we are no longer overtaken by our human frailties and instead see them with a vast view.

Loss of Old Drives and Preferences

When we are in a deeply spiritual transition we can lose interest in work, social interactions, and other life activities. We can feel lost when a familiar enthusiasm has vanished or we struggle to find the motivation to engage the world. This is a stage of awakening. It can last for a long time, and our old drives will not return in the same familiar forms. Peter was thirty-eight when he had an abrupt and intense energy awakening and psychic opening.

> I have been working in science publishing for most of my adult life. I lost my interest and ability to work, as I could not focus on reading emails and could not find the motivation to write. My interest in science was almost reduced to zero, as I couldn't see the relevance of it anymore. Before awakening, my belief in science and science publishing was because of its objective truth. I then experienced how irrelevant scientific ideas and any other rational concepts are when it comes down to holding truth or reality.

Peter moved to South America and opened a bed-and-breakfast, changing his lifestyle radically. Once his life felt satisfying and authentic again, he could slowly integrate his knowledge of science with his knowledge of nondual awakening.

Sometimes awakening is followed by synchronicities, events that pull us spontaneously into a new direction—as if everything is falling into place. But the opposite happens also: a long dry spell, or even a dark night of the soul, that can trigger loss of faith, a sense of failure, fear about the future, and insecurities. This is more likely to happen when we forcefully try to reconnect with previous sources of motivation in life, rather than embracing a new way of being. Jo was a professional woman in her fifties with a long career in education when she lost her drive to act.

> I don't have any physical problems or psychological issues. I'm just facing the end of my world as I knew it. I have come to understand that nothing in the world can make me happy. The world is in ashes, without a doubt, nothing there. I don't know how to proceed, so I have complete apathy. I get myself up every day and try to do things, take care of my body, and move about like I am living. But I have no feeling, no sense of joy or peace.

A dark night like Jo's marks a search within for more authentic expressions of our heart. We need to explore ways of living that feel aligned with the truths of awakening. We live in a culture that encourages us to be practical, pursue goals, and follow the norms. When conventional advice seems hollow, we are forced to dig deeper into our authentic nature to discover actions and ways of being that are right for us. A long period of quietude and simplicity leads us inward as we try new ways of meeting life, without attachment to results. We can connect to an inner voice that offers guidance and our direction can gradually become clearer. If we refuse to slow down, listen, and change courses, if we try to force things, we can experience disappointments, emotional challenges, and even physical illnesses. This challenge invites us to learn to express more intuitively and authentically, to listen to our heart and gut, and to act naturally in the moment.

Physical Issues

As we are awakening, strange things may happen to our body. We may feel disabled by erratic movements, pain, or discomfort in the stomach, neck, or back. Our big toe may hurt or the nail may fall off. We may feel overheated and get rashes. Sometimes the body purges for a few days as it eliminates toxins. Jonathan had many digestive problems while in India with his guru.

> My stomach would expand to the size of a bowling ball whenever I ate, I had constant belching and gas, and my vision was blurry and clouded. Yet doctors said nothing was wrong with me. I experienced incredible heat and burning in my body, as if I was on fire. I went to the emergency room several times fearing I was having a heart attack.

These conditions could certainly be evidence of gastrointestinal illness, but the doctors found nothing, so Jonathan regarded the physical symptoms as releases of energy that would ultimately be healing. His journey may have benefitted from probiotics and other digestive assistance. And his body may have needed a break from the intensity of his meditative practices.

One common complaint is pain in the neck and shoulders that has no medical cause. Energy is often blocked here, as we tense up with stress or by holding rigid positions while using computers or doing other tasks. The throat is also where we restrain self-expression and feelings. As I mentioned in the section on granthis, it's as if everything we've ever left unsaid gets trapped in the throat. When something outrageous happens, we can swallow our feelings to maintain an illusion of what it is to be spiritual: all-tranquil and all-forgiving. This is just a form of avoidance, because to be truly spiritual we need to face whatever arises. I met one man whose face twitched and jerked spontaneously but, once he released his anger in therapy at a wife who betrayed and abandoned him, these problems went away.

Pain, night sweats, and extreme shaking may arise because an old injury or emotional distress is finally releasing, or because toxins from alcohol or medications are moving out of our system. One client's jaw had been damaged long ago by dental work, and as he did energy practices his head began shaking. Another client, a recovered alcoholic, told me he would sweat so heavily that he had to change his bedsheets every night. Kundalini seems to work to remove anything held in the body that is damaged or unhealthy.

When physical difficulties are seriously impacting our life, it is helpful to take a break from meditation or energy practices. It is possible that overstimulation is causing shifts in hormone levels, depleting electrolytes, or damaging our nervous system. Consult with a naturopathic doctor, ayurvedic practitioner, nutritionist, or any allopathic specialist if physical discomforts persist.

Insomnia

Difficulty sleeping is the most common complaint from people in an awakening process. As soon as our body relaxes, energy rises. Our mind churns with concerns and we feel anxiety about what is going on. An estimated 50 to 70 million people in the US suffer from insomnia,[41] so it is difficult to say how much it is related to awakening and how much is due to modern lifestyles. People who meditate for long periods of time often need less sleep, but still they believe something is wrong if they can't sleep for seven or eight hours. In ashrams and zendos students often get up at 4 a.m. to enter deep meditation, and I've met people who do this spontaneously.

Energy can awaken us in the middle of the night and we can move involuntarily. Whether moving into yoga postures, hand gestures, shaking, jerking, or stretching, or even encountering sleep paralysis, try not to resist. Let the body release naturally. This will pass, as deep relaxation in sleep can trigger release and restructuring as part of a spiritual process.

We need some sleep each night to clear our brain. If we do not sleep at all for more than two nights, we may experience confusion, visions, erratic thoughts, and impulsive reactions similar to a mental illness like psychosis. These states will pass once we are rested. For this reason, if you are ever awake all night and cannot sleep the night after, take a sleep aid. I am occasionally awake all night long, and have learned to read, write, meditate, or watch television without concern. I just go to bed early the following night.

Insomnia is common, and there are many suggested remedies on the Internet, including relaxing audio recordings. I have found that avoiding electronic devices for two hours before bedtime is helpful, and also a simple practice of counting my breaths backward from one hundred. Avoid becoming angry and stressed about not sleeping because you can create an anxiety that makes it even more difficult. You could try rearranging your schedule to accommodate your sleep needs and the times of day when you feel most functional. Experiment with finding your natural rhythm, and know sleep is a foundation that may have shifted along with your energies.

Heightened Sensitivity

We can develop heightened sensitivity as we awaken. Some people can no longer go into large box stores or be in crowds, as their senses are too easily overwhelmed or they seem to absorb others' problems psychically. This absorption can cause feelings of nausea or illness, which is especially hard for anyone in a profession that involves working with people's pain and suffering. After a deep and insightful meditation retreat, Barbara returned to the world and encountered this.

Sensitivity has increased so that I take in others' feelings and emotions. This causes physical problems, mostly tension in the muscles of my back, arms, and legs. I also feel tired. Memory problems have increased at work, where I try unsuccessfully to follow very logical and technical discussions in a noisy environment.

An increase in sensitivity can cause us to realize a work environment doesn't fit any longer, or that certain people in our lives create stress, conflicting emotions, or reactivity. We may need to change our situation to be more congruent with our new way of being. Barbara chose to leave the stressful work environment and become a yoga teacher.

If we are doing something unhealthy for our mind, body, or spirit, we can suddenly feel it in ways we never noticed before. It is an unfortunate myth in some spiritual communities that if you are awake you have a capacity to tolerate anything. You may feel love and compassion for everyone, but that does not mean you can continue to be in environments or with people who are hostile or toxic. You may need to leave.

Sensitivity can increase so much it becomes hard to be in any social situation. We might become psychically sensitive, like Roberta.

I see spirit beings. I see the auras of trees and of humans, deceased and living, most of the time. I feel every emotion a person feels or is experiencing. It is overwhelming. I must avoid groups, crowds, and shopping.

When we're overwhelmed by sensitivity, it helps to think of ourselves as porous. If energy can enter our field, it can also move through it, and keep going into the universe. Instead of catching and holding feelings, let them move right through. They don't belong to us and we do not need them. Let them move on out, into the infinite sky.

Another type of sensitivity is heightened vision, smell, taste, touch, and sound. A classical scripture about kundalini describes how the senses can become so acute we might see ants crawling up a tree many yards away. Some people become aware of internal sounds, such as bees buzzing, kettledrums pounding, or bells ringing. Some hear chanting in a foreign language or the toning of *ohm*, which according to Vedanta is the sound of the universe. Vedanta describes this heightened sensual sensitivity as a great intimacy with everything that follows deep realization experiences. Here is Joelle's experience.

> *My senses were so enhanced I would stay in my room and touch the wall, fascinated by the subtle texture, for the whole evening. An hour would pass like ten minutes in the shower, where I could see every drop of water. I could stare at my hand, a blade of grass, or a candle, and be totally captivated. Listening to the wind blow the leaves outside my window was mesmerizing. I would see the same energy in everything: thousands of strands of light moving through living things and inanimate objects. The connectedness I feel in this state is profound, and also a little scary. When my ego kicks in, I feel almost too present, like I can't step back and find perspective on my experience. There is so much beauty and love in this state, but also fear.*

Another form of sensitivity is hearing the thoughts of someone else. Mindreading has been reported in stories of Tibetan lamas and Indian gurus. A modern Christian mystic and spiritual healer, Joel Goldsmith, reported an ability to hear the thoughts of others, and some who have followed his meditation practices for a long time also develop this capacity. Lanelle, one of his students, told me:

*This made having honest communication extremely difficult,
since people react badly to the possibility that you might know
their thoughts. My head was so full of thoughts belonging to
other people that I hated it and prayed for it to go away. The
ability did go away and has not returned.*

In a few people, particularly if there is a history of trauma, heightened sensitivity can release memories and emotions long repressed. We feel bombarded with experiences that pull up deep, unconscious material. Yet even while facing these painful emotions, underneath there can be a sense that all is well, love is here, and even happiness is arising. The Christian saints seem to carry this same complex mixture of suffering, love, and joy. Margo experienced this sensitivity for two years.

*I was aware of energies around me, whether from nature or
people. I was releasing a lot of emotional pain and felt emotions
I never felt before. When I saw someone on the street who
looked familiar to someone from my past, the release would
begin. But besides all the negativity and pain, I also had a loving
feeling I cannot describe. It was like floating or being in heaven.
There was missing a loved one, then there was love, and the
sense of loss dissipated.*

In some cases, heightened sensitivity can make us appear so out of balance that we are referred to medical attention and even hospitalization. When this happens, our psyche is too overwhelmed to cope and spiritual emergence has become an emergency, which is the topic of chapter 6. It can lead to a diagnosis, perhaps of posttraumatic stress disorder (PTSD) or a psychosomatic or conversion disorder. When we are this open and vulnerable, we may need conventional therapeutic support to work through a traumatic history.

Besides sensitivities of mind, the physical body can become highly sensitive. Invasive treatments, such as acupuncture, can feel hard to endure. It can impact sexuality and the ability to be in groups. Reactions to medications, toxins, and supplements can intensify. Practices such as qigong or kundalini yoga can occasionally raise so much energy that body heat becomes overwhelming.

When sensitivity is heightened, we need to moderate activities and pay attention to our reactivity. Often this means giving up practices that increase sensitivity. Pushing through reactions to reach some next level can burn out our energy system, lengthening the time needed to recuperate and balance. Instead, engage activities that feel calming and grounding. Listen deeply within, and avoid people and situations that are overwhelming. Instead of limiting our quality of life, heightened sensitivity can become an enhancement, enabling us to see radiant beauty in creation, enjoy quiet moments, and enrich our connections with others.

Visionary or Auditory Events

When kundalini is active in our body, energy may activate brain centers that make you vulnerable to visionary and auditory events. Kenneth was fifty-two when he experienced three days of clairvoyant and clairaudient experiences during a fast.

> *Shortly after my awakening, I took on the task of forgiving all who had ever harmed me. One night, I crossed my kitchen to turn off my boiling tea water. I clearly heard, "Get that tattoo artist away from my guitar player!" It sounded like it was coming from the teapot. Later that night, on my next trip to the newly-boiling teapot, I heard an otherworldly chant overlaid by a male voice babbling and talking about demons, the kingdom, and such. It was as beautiful and fascinating as it was shocking and terrifying. I was most relieved to pick up that boiling teapot and have the chanting end. Any form of white noise made it easier to hear sounds like these, whether it was the refrigerator, computer fan, forced air heater, or running water in the sink— all consistently turned up the volume.*

Kenneth's prior history of sound health meant that he could pull himself out of these altered states by eating, sleeping, and grounding himself. Kenneth needed to reorient himself with simple everyday activities, to stop fasting and isolating himself.

Designer drugs like LSD or plant medicines like ayahuasca and mushrooms also produce visual and auditory events. In his book *Hallucinations,* Oliver Sacks describes these possibilities from the perspective of neurological research.[42] He writes that many who have hallucinatory experiences are not psychotic, but the brain compensates by producing visions and language when normal pathways are not functioning, such as following a stroke or during long periods of sense deprivation—as occurs in deep meditation or fasting.

I believe that when intense energy strikes certain brain areas, it triggers visual and audio hallucinations that seem to come from other dimensions. In most cases, a person who is awakening experiences a positive or encouraging message such as "Peace be with you" or "It's really okay" or "Just keep practicing" that helps them face a difficult time.

Psychic Abilities

Psychic openings may also happen in a spiritual process, producing inner messages or precognitive dreams and visions. Melanie had this experience.

> I was driving to work when a voice in my head told me to drive to my father's home, a few miles out of my way. I argued with the impulse but it kept arising, so finally I went to his house—and discovered he had just had a stroke and fell to the floor. I was able to get him to a hospital and saved his life.

Other clients have told me they had periods of time when they were able to:

⊛ perceive others' thoughts or emotions;

- ⊛ see catastrophic events in visions, before they happen;

- ⊛ read the past lives, or future experiences, of other people;

- ⊛ see a world event, such as a tsunami, while it is happening;

- ⊛ sense great upheaval going on somewhere in the world;

- ⊛ receive visitations from deceased family members of friends and acquaintances;

- ⊛ sense the passing of a loved one and feel connected psychically as he or she leaves the body;

- ⊛ or visit with a recently deceased person who offers information needed by other family members.

The ability to predict the future can bring great concern along with it, because we can feel we are responsible to warn others, yet the likelihood of being taken seriously is slim. Usually, psychic abilities pass, or occur rarely in our life, but a strong intuitive sense does become more stable after awakening energy and consciousness. Intuition is subtler than psychic ability, and usually more personal.

Energetic Activity in the Head

Yogis say that opening the crown area of our head begins a dissolution of the sense of a personal self. Uncomfortable sensations in the crown include the feeling of being drilled or operated on, buzzing or popping noises and other disturbing sounds, and a temporary feeling that we cannot concentrate or think as clearly as we used to. There is no set pattern to these phenomena, as they can happen while in meditation, reciting mantras, trying to sleep, or doing daily activities. Janice found her energy spontaneously moved around her head.

I see lots of color when meditating or closing my eyes.
Sometimes flashes of white light swirl around, but mainly

shades of purple, violet, blue. I hear lots of crackling in my
head, like popping noises.

Thomas described waking up late at night, feeling half asleep and relaxed until he entered the bathroom, turned on the light, and shut the door.

I suddenly and without warning felt an intense buzzing,
vibrating, energetic force low in my back that blasted up though
my spine and straight out the top of my head—giving off an
intense, bluish-white light, like lightning. It was overwhelming,
but there was no pain. The buzzing was loud and otherworldly.
The light seemed as bright as the sun, but did not hurt my eyes.
My body shook from the unimaginable power coursing through
it. I was simultaneously overcome with a level of primal fear and
terror that I did not know a human being could experience. The
moment seemed to transcend time and space, being ancient and
beyond description.

As dramatic as these encounters are in the moment, they pass, and we recover. When we have an attitude of surrender, energy can move all the way through, which allows great peace and insight to flood mind and body. Life goes on and even returns to an ordinary rhythm, with a changed perspective.

Jana Dixon, author of *Biology of Kundalini*, believes that solar and lunar cycles, climate and atmospheric conditions, the seasons, and the energy of the earth all impact the pressure or pulsing of energy in our head. They can trigger the tinnitus and vertigo sometimes reported when kundalini is awakened. She has found that people who have opened their energetic field are more responsive to these universal conditions than the average person. To reduce reactivity to nature's vibrational forces, she recommends long walks by rivers, lying on the grass, and avoiding dairy products.[43]

If energies in the head are not moving, but feel circular and repetitive and uncomfortable, imagine energy flowing from the head to the heart or to the center of your body in the belly. Changing a meditation practice so that it is more grounding and centering can also help balance energy so that it is not so intensely concentrated in our head.

Out-of-Body Experiences

During awakening moments, consciousness can seem to move free of our body—whether we observe our own physical activity from a distance, are plunged into vast dimensions of space, or become a diffuse and etheric essence without boundary. Blake was a college student whose spiritual quest took him to India, where he asked the guru Satya Sai Baba for initiation into the Gayatri mantra.[44]

> A few days later, I was safely tucked in bed, chanting the Gayatri mantra till I started to nod off. The next thing I knew, I was consciously leaving my body and floating upward above my bed, the house, the city, the earth, ever upward until I was flying freely through the universe in my perfected form. When I say "perfected form," it was the form I have now, only perfect in every way, dazzling with brilliant light and energizing sparks. After some time, I started falling back to earth very quickly. I fell into a deep pit on the earth's surface and kept descending until I hit a huge, sleeping serpent or dragon of some kind. I was frightened, as I intuitively felt this creature was very powerful. The serpent chased me up and out of the abyss, and let out a mighty roar that I can't describe in words. Next thing I knew, I found myself back in bed with a racing heart and sweaty body. I continued to chant the Gayatri mantra till sleep took me over.

Although it may seem unlikely to Western minds, in Eastern traditions repeating *mantras*—which are spiritually potent words, phrases, or sounds—can have powerful effects that include transcendent and visionary states. Many people feel anxiety about out-of-body experiences, which may also happen spontaneously in response to emotional stress, as a half-awake dream state, during surgery, in life-threatening situations, and as a teachable skill known as *astral travel* or *remote viewing*. This capacity can be learned, so it is less a spiritual gift and more of a latent human potential not commonly developed. While we can be tempted to decide these transcendent states are evidence of awakening, they often do not lead to self-realization. Instead, they exhibit the range of consciousness. Once the drama and excitement are over, we still need to understand *who* or *what* is aware of every experience, both transcendent and mundane. If the excitement produces a longing for more and more adventures, realization remains elusive. Awakening is about finding what never changes—and all experiences change.

Heart Openings

Every tradition has ways of opening our heart and expanding our capacity to love, whether through ritual, worship, devotion, or chants. Some people feel their hearts open through relationships with gurus, and Christian saints describe overwhelming love for Jesus. Our hearts can also open by falling in love, sometimes irrationally or without any hope of reciprocation. The heart also breaks open with grief.

The heart can be a powerful portal into realizing our true nature, as a heart opening can lead to dramatic shifts in our energy and worldview. It is an intensely physical and emotional experience as all armoring around our heart breaks down. It opens the contractions around our heart that we formed in our early years. This also has risks.

Love arises when we are touched deeply by someone, and this can make us vulnerable to a spiritual teacher who cannot contain sexual energy. Any therapist is aware that, because he or she may be the first person to ever deeply listen to and value a client, the client may fall in love. In psychology, there are licensing ethics that forbid romantic or sexual liaisons with clients. But in spirituality, the boundaries are not so clear. If love arises and a teacher exploits a student by engaging in a sexual relationship, it can derail spiritual process by personalizing what is actually a deep awakening to *being* love, rather than *needing* love. When teachers misuse this connection for personal satisfaction, they do a great disservice to their community. Christine's description of her experience of love for her teacher offers another way to approach it.

> *I felt an overwhelming love for my teacher after a profound realization and awakening in his presence during a retreat. For weeks, it poured through me and my body became so alive and full of joy whenever I saw him. As a therapist, I was well aware of this experience as a process, and of my own need to open my heart. Since he was young enough to be my son, I felt comfortable telling him how I felt. I even apologized for being such a gushing idiot around him. He laughed and said he would hold the projection for me until I was able to own it myself. In time, the intensity faded into a sweet affection and gratitude, and the desire to be around him dissolved. I recognized I was experiencing my own self. I believe any true teacher will turn this energy back to its source.*

Opening the heart is a great blessing in the awakening process, and if respected the experiences that arise do not lead to a crisis. If we understand that the feelings, sensations, and emotions are part of a heart opening, we can consider them to be catalysts for our benefit that operate alongside our own aspirations. When there is no underlying psychological imbalance or projection onto another person, each step can be navigated with relative ease. The journey produces gratitude, insight, and relaxation within unconditional loving. Mystics across traditions emphasize the role of the heart in self-realization, and the discovery that awakening itself is an experience of love.

Ultimately, We Are Alone in Awakening

It is rare to find a spiritual advisor or a health provider who is familiar with what we are going through, and our family may seem bewildered. Misinterpretations are common. Many who teach yoga, qigong, meditation, Christian contemplation, martial arts, shamanism, Reiki, network chiropractic, Internet courses, and other practices that can activate kundalini, know very little about the spiritual awakening process. A few have called me in a panic when kundalini energy arose, and some even want help making it go away. Gopi Krishna wrote a groundbreaking book about his own experiences in 1960, when he could find no one in India who could help him. Many who awaken this energy have no one to turn to for help, and no paradigm that can be used to explain what is happening other than illness. Usually the people we turn to for guidance have the same limitations.

Doctors may prescribe heavy medications that exacerbate the problems or create new ones. We can encounter unnecessary hospitalizations and assumptions that we are mentally ill or physically disabled. This can come from allopathic or alternative practitioners alike: one man I spoke with was told by an acupuncturist that he needed to be hospitalized and given oxygen treatments to alleviate his symptoms. This is not the fault of the medical system. We are painfully missing a paradigm for the process of adjusting to spiritual awakening. During a summer internship, Margo participated in some Shamanic practices at an Indian reservation. When she told her dad, a psychiatrist, about these experiences, he said she was crazy and insisted she come home and be institutionalized. He accused her of being a loser who wanted to drop out of college.

I was afraid that I'd do something drastic and I didn't trust myself, but I stayed in school. There was no one I could talk to about it. After my talk with my dad, I forced myself to forget it and committed what I call "emotional suicide" by stuffing it all down, deep inside. This was followed by a major depression. The next year I went back to the reservation and told one of the women who lived there about it. She told me that it sounded like spirit was trying to break free.

It is worth a search for supportive professionals, because many can offer useful techniques for balance even when they don't have the complete picture. When you make inquiries of a provider, ask if they have an interest in Eastern spirituality, an understanding of energy release and grounding, or an openness to alternative healing. A few doctors and therapists are trained in, or have personally had, transpersonal experiences. They may be able to support you physically and emotionally through this process. Use discrimination about who you choose to work with.

Being Awake in a Sleeping World

Living in an awakened state in the world invites us into a paradoxical mystery: we feel alone, yet at one with every living thing. We live in a world where we are constantly bombarded with opinions, positions, fear-based commercialism, and models that demonstrate how we should eat, dress, interact with peers, perform our roles in life, and even think. It isn't easy to find our unique way and trust our self when burdened with all these messages.

We also live in a world filled with churches. As organizations, they have gained great influence by convincing large groups of people to follow one belief and to lean on a hierarchy in which the upper tier is the sole interpreter of spiritual wisdom, the sole source of guidance. This presents a challenge for any believer who feels the inner urge to seek truth, who has questions about just what the nature of God is, who is curious about exploring the meaning of life. This personal, independent search has been condemned as heresy and many great mystics were outcasts, even martyrs, in their time. All because they saw beyond the boundaries of the religion or culture they had trusted.

A true awakening breaks us out of all systems, all conventions, and all need for blind faith. The result is an isolating experience. We personally encounter the mysteries of an existence that is infinite, unbounded, without concept, and free from judgment. The tragedy of the human addiction to concepts, and conceptual ways of under-standing existence, becomes apparent.

It can be a horrific shock to discover this is a lens ignored by most of the population. Spiritual awakenings take us out of the status quo, out of living in complacency. We see that many social patterns are pretense. They are not wrong, they are just not real. We see how people live from their egos, centered on personal desires and aversions, and are clearly separated from the deepest understanding of their own true self. And as a result, we can be labeled strange, rebellious, uncooperative, or even mentally ill by our friends, family, neighbors, pastors, medical professionals, and therapists, who might know better if they only had a paradigm for recognizing our experi-ence and vision. This can lead to subtle or extreme feelings of alienation.

When we understand the reasons for these challenges and open to the changes they bring, we can find our center. Some teachers have even said we are on the edge of an evolution of human con-sciousness, so we find ourselves frequently in unknown territory. If we can trust that this is a process occurring for our benefit and find a quiet core of acceptance and peace, we can effectively support our self during this transitional time. We need to address these chal-lenges, not by racing to find an expert to cure us, rather by finding a silent witness within, and an interior capacity to love and support our self. We need to take care of our body and create a nurturing environment as free of stress as possible. And we may need to stand up against negative thinking about awakening, both in our self and in others.

6. Emergence, Emergency, or Mental Illness

The challenges we face in a spiritual emergence can become an emergency. At times, feelings of crises are simply reactions to events that are frightening and hard to interpret. Depending on our attitudes and beliefs, prior functioning and health, and level of anxiety, the intensity of an awakening can cause us to be unable to function in our life. Using psychedelic substances or surviving a traumatic event can trigger a brief emergency because we are temporarily disoriented. In some cases, spiritual emergence becomes an emergency because a psychiatrist judges a non-ordinary state of consciousness to be a mental illness, and uses medications or hospitalization to suppress the experience. Research suggests hundreds of people annually are misdiagnosed and inappropriately treated.[45] This was what happened to Bridgett, a psychologist in London who had an awakening after a near-death experience during childbirth.

A big light first came into my hands and then into my belly. A powerful energy came into my womb that was stronger than giving birth. I quickly got into my bed and then the energy exploded into my heart. I was shaking all over, with big contractions. I thought I was dying from a heart attack. The energy came into my head and then there was this big silence. There was just "it." The voice of a teacher from India who had passed away came into my head. "Am I dead?" I asked him. He said, "Well, there is no difference between life and death. You are just so attached to your body." I asked where I was. He said, "You are in the now!" I felt miserable. Then there was this beautiful female voice. I saw the sweetest mother face I had ever seen. It was God in a female way. She said, "Now you know you need to surrender." When I told

my husband, he called the weekend doctor and they put me
in an ambulance and took me to a psychiatric clinic.

Bridgett was hospitalized, diagnosed, and medicated, which confused her. For years, she feared her vulnerability to insanity and she feared spiritual practice. Like many others who are inappropriately diagnosed, she felt shattered by this response to something that, to her, was a sacred experience.

Emergencies That Find Resolution

B. S. Goel was a young man in India studying for his PhD in philosophy. He was practicing yoga and meditation, had an awakening that could have become an emergency, but was supported in an appropriate way. He tells his story in *Third Eye and Kundalini*.

A great energy force rose from the base of my spine and rushed up to the crown of the head, where Hindus keep a lock of hair. I noticed further that the force which went up to that point also removed something from that point which looked like a cork on a bottle. And lo! I stood there a completely transformed man in a high state of ecstasy! My vision changed immediately and the total world assumed a silvery white shape. My friend told me that even the color of my face became crimson.[46]

Goel describes many of his subsequent spiritual experiences in his book, including a kundalini arising that he felt happened through the grace of his guru. But he also felt many symptoms of "mental diseases" arise during his awakening process. These included extreme confusion, anxiety neurosis with reactive depression, paranoia with religious delusions, auditory and visual hallucinations, manic-depressive states, drowsy states, schizoid trends, insomnia, extreme restlessness, and delirium. His brother was a psychiatrist who monitored Goel with his spiritual practices and intentions in mind. Goel says he was very fortunate that he never followed psychiatric treatment because, once energy opened his third eye, he had no doubt about the spiritual nature of his experience. He was able to navigate the challenges of awakening without ever veering into a diagnosed emergency.

Carmela's story shows how an emergence can briefly become an emergency before resolving itself. She was a young woman in Mexico when her family became so alarmed about her emotional state that she was taken to a psychiatrist.

> *I was overtaken by episodes of intense rage and confusion,*
> *then suddenly having peace, bliss, and outbursts of compassion*
> *and oneness with everything in the world. Then the next*
> *moment I was crying and laughing without any reason.*
> *Within two or three days, I was almost mad, so my parents*
> *decided to take me to a psychiatrist. But later that same night,*
> *I was relaxing in bed when suddenly a white light—like a*
> *bullet—came from the base of my spine and exploded in my*
> *brain. It was marvelous and indescribable. It was like I was in*
> *an ocean of light and consciousness, feeling that I am God, or*
> *I am in a consciousness like God. I was immersed in that for*
> *some time and then slowly I returned to my body*
> *consciousness and felt complete calm.*

This is a common situation. Behavior can become so uncharacteristic that family members see a breakdown happening and seek psychiatric care. In Carmela's case, when the intensity of emotion calmed, she began a slow process of assimilating both positive and negative feelings. She needed a calm and nurturing home environment in which she could reduce stress and take her time working through underlying issues in her life.

A spiritual emergency can pass with rest, support, and understanding the nature of spiritual awakening. If dramatic events pass quickly, we can become more relaxed about the process as we learn to understand it and make life changes. Unfortunately, without proper support difficult phenomena can endure for very long periods of time, until everyday functioning is impaired, our body feels weakened, and our spirit becomes depressed. An emergency can become a long-term illness of energy and spirit.

When Spiritual Emergency Is Diagnosed as Mental Illness

Lawrence was a recent high school graduate traveling in India when he encountered a spiritual teacher for the first time. During two weeks with this teacher, his chest felt very tight, he sensed an energy flow around his body and in his spine, and he experienced hot and cold rushes, movement, and shaking.

> *This energy became an explosion in my brain that, in a few days, became a tsunami. It came in through the top of my head, producing an astoundingly big expansion in consciousness that seemed to encompass the whole of the universe. I was incredibly afraid and thought I was going to physically die. The boundaries and limitations between me and the rest of the world faded away. It felt like I was having a big spiritual psychotic breakdown, because all I could see and feel around me was this empty space of energy that was shaking and roaring. I also felt incredible pain, like needles piercing through my body, and could not sleep for two nights.*

In this state, Lawrence roamed the city until the police found him and brought him back to where he was staying. He ate practically nothing and became very weak. Because he seemed unable to take care of himself, friends took him to a hospital where he was given a diagnosis of schizophrenia and medications.

When we have an opening of this sort, and are considered mentally ill, we may spend years doubting our sanity, and always be fearful of spiritual practices. Instead of entering a process of awakening, our identity can contract and we become limited by a diagnosis. This inhibits our capacity to feel safe in the world. Spiritual emergency needs to be better known so that we have a more positive paradigm for interpreting our experiences.

The dramatic events that can accompany awakening are often misunderstood by helping professionals. This is because many of the phenomena are similar to diagnostic criteria for some mental illnesses. It is also extremely rare for therapists or doctors to be exposed to spiritual literature as part of their training. In recent years diagnostic standards have undergone an evolution toward improving treatment, reducing harm from misdiagnosis, and increasing clinical training to address the spiritual dimension of human experience,[47] but there is still far to go. We do now have a diagnostic code that does not pathologize spiritual awakening, and simply places it on a list of life issues that are sometimes addressed in therapy. Even so, in the diagnostic manual, there remains no depth to the description that would help an interviewer determine whether a client is in a psychiatric crisis or a spiritual awakening.

The vagueness in differentiating spiritual emergence and spiritual emergency from mental illness often contributes to a pathological diagnosis such as bipolar, schizophrenia, or conversion disorder. All have conventional, if not necessarily effective, medical treatments. When experiencers are treated with medications, hospitalizations, and the misperception that they are mentally ill, they may feel stigmatized for years afterward. Unless the focus is on rest, healthy food, protection, calming techniques, and supportive discussions with an understanding therapist, hospitalization will not help. Many people I have known who were hospitalized realized early on that their symptoms were situational, refused heavy medication, knew they were not permanently disabled, and pulled themselves together to gain an early release.

Dr. Stanislov Grof and his wife, Christina Grof, did pioneering work in the field of spiritual emergence during the 1980s. They collected hundreds of cases of spiritual emergency that were misdiagnosed as mental illnesses, and held conferences designed to help health professionals learn about this important aspect of human experience. Today the International Spiritual Emergence Network, ISEN, lists licensed professionals all over the world who are qualified to assist people in spiritual emergency.[48]

Emergence, Emergency, or Mental Illness?

It is often said in meditation communities that we need to benefit from a healthy ego before awakening in order to navigate meditation and awakening successfully. Paradoxically, after awakening it is easier to release a self you knew and now see as irrelevant than it is to live with an awakening in which you never knew or enjoyed who you were pretending to be. Good self-care is the best way to navigate awakening, with a moderate lifestyle and a willingness to clean up bad habits, go to counseling to resolve painful memories, and consciously change dysfunctional beliefs and patterns.

Experiences of extraordinary phenomena do not necessarily indicate a mental illness. From my experience with clients, I have observed that there are ways to differentiate between spiritual emergence, emergency, and mental illness. Here are elements to consider.

Evidence of Functioning Before Awakening

Traditionally, students were not accepted into Eastern spiritual communities unless they had a relatively healthy family background and personal history, a strong focus on spirituality, and a proclivity for good self-discipline. Today all practices, even the most advanced, are readily available to everyone. If we are suffering from low self-esteem or unresolved traumas from childhood, entangled in toxic or abusive relationships, and generally have not taken good care of our bodies, then any awakening process will be more challenging. The process is disorienting since more issues come to the surface demanding more change.

Even with a solid ego structure, spiritual emergency occurs more commonly in people with physical or sexual abuse in their backgrounds, serious deprivations in childhood, or PTSD from other traumatic events. Deep meditation does tend to trigger old memories and emotions so they surface. If you activate kundalini energy to clear out blockages, the memories and sensations of the earlier trauma will arise. Also a history of drug or alcohol abuse may make us vulnerable. I believe this is because subtle damages and residual toxins get released in energetic movements as we heal. Anything that makes an awakening more psychologically disruptive, brings up old suffering, or causes releases to be more intense, can lead to spiritual emergency. There are exceptions: not everyone with trauma goes into emergency, just as many with these histories can lead productive and contented lives. Other factors, such as sensitivity, genetics, supportive life influences, and personality style also impact how we engage our awakenings.

When assessing yourself, or someone else, to determine between spiritual emergence and mental illness, consider self-care and social interaction before the triggering event. Usually a person who is psychotic or bipolar has a poor history before the energetic awakening, so afterward there is also difficulty with depression, mood swings, delusions, relationships, employment, social anxiety, or confusion between the relative world and what's happening in their head. He or she may have been impulsive, withdrawn, paranoid, or depressive long before the reported spiritual event. This is the structure we use to function in the world. Was there a sense of personal self that functioned?

The vast majority of people who are awakening spiritually do not have a mental illness—they are often educated professionals who report supportive relationships. They are clear about the difference between prior functioning and what they've been experiencing since the anomalous events. If they have traumatic experiences in their past, they have addressed them in therapy and are not afraid to face them. They may be young people, without much life experience, who triggered awakening and have no context to put it in. These factors can all indicate they are not mentally ill, just temporarily impacted by circumstances.

Level of Negativity, Dark Images, Anger, Fear, and Confusion

The emergence process is more likely to become an emergency when we are overcome by fear or mental confusion, or we rage at the changes being demanded of us. We all have different tolerances for pain and different expectations about having control in our lives. The process is impacted by how tightly we hold to our image of normalcy, demanding that life stay the same. The shifts of energy and consciousness can cause us to feel out of control, so our level of tolerance and flexibility is important.

A small percent of people experience dark or foreboding images, which often trigger an emergency. This seems more common in people with traumatic histories and substance addictions, and in people who do tantric and shamanic practices that deliberately induce darkness to relate with shadowy or evil aspects of human consciousness.

> *Nan was limited to a wheelchair because of childhood polio, and she lived with her mother in an eighth-floor apartment in Manhattan. One day, a yogi visited her home and initiated her in his lineage, telling her that she would be healed. Afterward she began seeing "demons" outside her windows, which tormented her. She tried to get help from his organization, but they ignored her calls and she never saw the yogi again.*

It is possible these images represented her rage at fate and her life's limitations. They may have become personified after energy was stimulated and entered the area of her brain that produces hallucinations. I believe it is often repressed rage, misery, or past terrors that generate fearful images and voices in our heads. As discussed in chapter 5, visions or hallucinations may be stimulated by sense deprivation or specific brain activity.

If dark and menacing images arise, and there is persistent confusion between thoughts, projections, or visions and what is actually happening around us, this can be a spiritual emergency or a more serious psychological break with reality. If the symptoms persist and interfere with peace of mind or the ability to function, then psychiatric intervention is important.

Usually the energies of awakening are strange and unfamiliar, but they are rarely extremely emotionally painful. If you are unable to sleep for a long period, become too influenced by psychic voices or entities, or feel such pain you are overwhelmed, you may be slipping into a psychiatric disorder. Depending on your prior history, this may or may not be a temporary condition, but you need help to overcome it. Awakening is not about getting caught in other-dimensions or worlds, or feeling disabling pain. It is about a deep stillness and inner light that enhances, rather than diminishes, life. It is about clarity and love. Get help when you need it so you are not stuck in crippling detours.

Duration of Extreme Psychological or Emotional Symptoms

When awakening, it is natural to have occasional stretches of brain fog, loss of interest, and emotional release that you do not understand. You may feel an intuitive impulse to be in a certain place, or try something new, or follow a new passion for creative activity that seems to just flow through you. You may feel huge waves of joy and unconditional love, followed by a great let-down a few days later.

If these issues continue for weeks and others comment on your mania, suggest you are out of control, or say they think you may be in danger, take time to be quietly present with yourself. Write out what you are experiencing, reflect on what is important to you, and do the grounding practices described in the next chapter. You might also benefit from working with a compassionate therapist. Even feeling tempted to act out in ways that are harmful to yourself or others is a sign of needing psychological support. Seek professional help if you have repeated, lengthy periods of mental confusion when your mind is not functioning in useful ways. Mood swings that are intense enough to frighten others indicate a crisis you cannot resolve alone.

You do not need to be mentally ill to face issues that disrupt your life in these ways. The power of the awakening process can bring up conditions that have been latent or well-controlled in the past. They come up to be resolved and healed. If you never saw it, you could not address it. This is an opportunity to move beyond your ingrained conditioning to create a more authentic life.

Identification with Phenomena

A few people who experience awakenings find their ego is owning the content of the experience. A healthy ego is a sense of identity that feels blessed or humbled by a sacred vision or experience of grace, but does not own it. It might be overwhelmed with joy or reactive with fear when the experience passes. When we watch an extraordinary sunrise, we feel awe but we know we do not own the sun.

Yes, it is true, many who awaken deeply or teach about awakening will say they are God, that all of us are God. They feel dissolved in this contact with the indescribable, infinite source. They feel so intimate with all things that their understanding of what God means shifts. This is not the same as ego taking over this identification, which would make you, the little "me," feel special or better or wiser than everyone else.

The past identifications of ego begin to crumble after such a realization, but the mind can easily regroup with a new structure and claim a new identity. We can lose our ability to witness and discriminate. This is why a healthy ego structure prior to awakening is useful: it knows the ego (the separate sense of "me") cannot be God. Realization reveals something beneath ego that is unfathomable and eternal. "Me" is just a reflection, or movement, of light and energy with a unique appearance. It is not real in the *absolute* nature of things, while still being real as a form dancing among world appearances.

In a psychotic break, a person's ego or mind identifies with phenomena. This results in many interpretive distortions, including believing others are lying if they do not agree. Anger may arise quickly as well as demands that others uphold the person's position. There can be destructive acting out. B.S. Goel writes that the main difference between a madman and a person passing through a kundalini process is that "the former is the actor in the madness, and the latter often acts as a witness to his madness and hence remains unaffected by madness."[49]

Erratic Behaviors That Cause Chaos

Impulsively and periodically doing things that cause chaos, such as using drugs, spending money you don't have on items you don't need, stirring up fights, standing on corners to yell at people, or threatening suicide indicate you may be struggling with a mental illness. These are common factors in bipolar disorder and other psychiatric issues that are very unlikely to be caused by a spiritual awakening. It is possible that, if you have a mental illness, you may have expansive moments of insight or releases of energy, but it is not the awakening causing your chaotic behavior. When drugs are involved, it may be a drug reaction that will shift with sobriety.

On the other hand, if your life has been stable until after a triggering event and you feel an impulse to move or make changes that seem irrational to others, it may be a natural consequence of awakening. Awakening includes an impulse to become more congruent and authentic to your true nature. This is why prior history and the ability to take care of yourself are important factors to consider before jumping to a psychiatric diagnosis.

Spiritual Experiences Within Mental Illness

Episodes of mental illness may include spiritual experiences, but these are not useful spiritual events unless they can support healing and insight. Chaotic energy may arise and also spiritual images—such as visions of God, Jesus, Mary, Buddha, Krishna or other figures—but if they are the result of mental illness, they will amplify thought distortions rather than bring us to the deeper peace and clarity that a spiritual awakening offers. Here is what happened to Ted.

Ted stood up in an airplane and heard a voice saying God wanted him to walk down the aisle loudly blessing people. So he did. The seatbelt sign was on, flight attendants asked him to sit down, and he refused. He felt like he was experiencing a spiritual awakening, but he also had an injury to his head from falling off a freight train, had unresolved emotional trauma from early childhood losses, and he consistently smoked marijuana, including when doing meditation and Siddha Yoga practices. His thinking was not clear, he was causing chaos with behavior that was inappropriate for the situation, and he needed psychiatric support. He was arrested and taken to the hospital.

An awakened mind might feel like giving blessings to others, but knows this can cause problems on an airplane. A discriminating mind might do it silently. When psychosis is present, people can make serious and dangerous mistakes. They often do need protection from their erratic impulses. Spirituality can become a danger when it is overtaken by mental illness. Some indications that mental illness has overtaken spirituality include:

- The particular path or experience becomes a personal obsession and "insights" are aggressively imposed on others

- Conviction of possession by evil or satanic forces, or belief that others are so possessed

- Inflated beliefs of being God, a supreme being, or prophet with a special mission that makes one individual better than others

- Fascination with experiences of other dimensions to the detriment of living an ordinary life and caring for basic human needs

- When intuition or inner voice become externalized to an extent that it is frequently experienced as hallucinations

- Chaotic lifestyle

People with a mental illness can experience spiritual openings like anyone else and these may offer valuable insight or comfort. But spirituality should not be a reason to evade the psychiatric care that can help heal or manage behaviors that limit happiness and effectiveness in the world. Not to say that all psychiatric care is done right, only that there is sometimes a need for evaluation, help, and protection that includes cautious use of medications.

The problem is, psychiatry doesn't understand the process of spiritual awakening. It is not part of training and our medical culture is blind to subtlety. Patient groups, as well as transpersonal psychiatrists like Stanislav Grof, advocate moving away from complete dependence on medications, toward repairing splits in our psyche that arise from childhood trauma and neglect, or society's violence, inequities, and prejudices. They demand that the profession respect a wider variation of personal differences in lifestyle, ethnic, and social backgrounds rather than lumping everyone into an ideal of what's normal. If this happened and diverse ethnic and spiritual practices were better understood, recognizing spiritual emergence would be easier.

Opening Through Transitional Images

The most disorienting challenge of spiritual awakening, which can make us wonder if we are mentally ill, is when occasional visions arise. If you have experienced this, remember that visions have been known for centuries to occur in the lives of spiritual seekers and those known to be seers. In Western culture, this has become associated with mental illness simply because it is not common, and because psychosis also may include seeing images in the mind.

A vision of a spiritual figure sometimes appears when consciousness opens. Jesus, Mother Mary, Buddha, Paramahansa Yogananda, or Ramana Maharshi often show up. Aside from spiritual entities, we may become aware of the presence of someone who has passed away, or feel visited by a personal guide or guru—living or dead.

Some have a vision of an animal. We may see a story unfold or experience vivid déjà vu. These are basically waking dreams.

Images like these have the potential to help us align with a spiritual intention, receive helpful guidance and support, or open us to a new dimension. I think of these images as *transitional objects* that arise from the collective unconscious to support awakening. I call them "transitional" because it is easier for us to accept God in a human-like form than it is to awaken to the vast, omnipresent, eternal essence within it. Our minds can relate to it more easily. Until consciousness is ready to let go of attachment to form, we are gifted with images that represent sacred qualities or principles.

Traditional yogis might explain visions by saying that we were connected to the particular character or teacher in a prior life, or perhaps he or she represents a lineage connection. Visions arise in people doing Holotropic Breathwork, past-life regressions, and during psychedelic drug use or NDEs. They also occur spontaneously or during intense meditative states. A poet named Robert Adams once wrote that a little man would visit him as a child and sit at the edge of his bed to talk with him. He later recognized this man as Ramana Maharshi. The non-dual sage Papaji said that Krishna, a Hindu god, frequently came to play with him as a child.

In a spiritual awakening, these visions are rarely dark, foreboding, or repetitive. Entities in a spiritual vision will not recommend that we harm our self or anyone else, and they do not trigger paranoid ideation. If these things happen, and are not related to drugs or plant substances, you likely need therapeutic assistance. The fine line between spiritual awakening and psychosis can be navigated if we consider that psychotic experiences can arise temporarily when we use drugs, become too energetically stimulated to sleep for several nights, or fast in an effort to purify. If visions result from these causes, they will clear up shortly and will not return once we are free of toxins and fully rested. If visions arise repeatedly, professional help is needed.

Facing Fearful Archetypes

Frightening images may also be archetypal, coming from the collective field and history of humanity. They are not meant to be integrated in the way spiritual archetypes are; rather, we can see them as fearful or angry aspects of ourselves that need recognition and healing if the human species is to reach a kinder and more humane level of evolution. It is possible that people who seem to be mentally ill are highly sensitive and carry unconscious aspects of our culture, which uses violence to entertain and is even willing to kill other humans. These acts and images are considered acceptable under the guise of war over principles, and even as entertainment, but insane when they cause internal disruption. Sometimes spiritual awakening holds all the incongruence and paradox of the human condition. The conflicts described in the *Bhagavad-Gita*, a timeless Indian epic, illustrate this struggle to come to terms with darkness. Many spiritual seekers in India study it thoroughly.

In some cases, an extremely frightening vision arises because of unresolved psychological issues, often from terrifying early childhood experiences that were never put into words because the mind was not able to understand them at the time. It is possible that some people hold these memories from previous lives, in DNA, or ancestral memory. Tibetans believe that if a dark entity appears you may have conjured it up in a previous life; you must stand up to it and tell it you no longer want anything to do with it. Fear amplifies an experience of darkness, so it's helpful to find ways to shift focus by turning on the lights, getting a cup of tea, turning on soothing music, standing up to it, laughing at it, or calling a friend.

If you have repeated fearful experiences, work with a therapist to get to the core of the pattern that is causing them to arise. You might discover a part of you that has been neglected and can be awakened and redeemed. It is important to avoid dabbling in black magic, horror films, and dark interpretations of energy that you might find on the Internet. Many people refrain from watching news programs for a time.

If you are doing shamanic practices and spending time in the underworld, it is easy to trigger these difficult forms of energy. Although certain adventurous personality types can navigate these investigations with the support of a wise guide and teacher, they are not especially useful in the spiritual journey unless you intend to become a shaman. They can cause psychological distress in some personality types, especially those who have an abusive history.

A small percentage of people are plunged unexpectedly into challenging images of dismemberment or other disabling dreams and visions following a spontaneous awakening. Because such openings are disorienting, they can be traumatic. Psychiatrists may interpret these kinds of events as psychotic experiences because they have no understanding of shamanic traditions. The availability of support for shamanic expertise is extremely limited and differentiating a shamanic event from a psychotic opening is challenging. Both can carry very frightening imagery and visions from the deep unconscious. It may be helpful to study writings by shamans or seek someone in your community who has this background and understanding. It is a form of spiritual emergence that can lead to a deep transformation if properly guided.

Indications That Spiritual Events Are Not Symptoms of Mental Illness

I rarely consider spiritual events to indicate mental illness, especially if people meet the following criteria.

- They functioned reasonably well in the world, with work and relationships, before an awakening.

- There is no history of a psychiatric disorder or personality disorder.

- They can witness, rather than identify with, images and visions that arise, feeling alarm or curiosity rather than overwhelm.

⊛ They had prior interest in spiritual seeking and practices.

⊛ They can self-reflect on their history and patterns they wish to change.

⊛ There is positivity about the experience, with bliss or beneficial shifts in perspective, in which they feel okay despite the oddness of the events.

In these circumstances we can have a transient experience in which thought patterns undergo great change, but they are not psychotic. If the experience was preceded by drug use, days without sleep, or a serious trauma, then the symptoms are likely to pass once we are rested and have returned to daily life.

Many people become very disturbed about a single vision or hearing an inner voice because they believe only psychosis produces these effects. I have seen that this is not true, as anomalous events are far more frequent than people imagine. They often occur in times of stress, in the wildness of nature, with sleep deprivation, in meditation, and during or after using drugs or medications. They are not inevitable, nor are they an indicator of spiritual awakening. They are simply phenomena that occur in some people and not in others, depending on things like individual history, genetics, intensity of kundalini energy, and neurodynamic brain patterns. I have known many sane people who have occasional visions. And genuinely psychic people have ways of knowing what is happening that the rest of the population does not have. There is a vast mystery in the range of human experience.

Overcoming Spiritual Emergency with Tender-Loving Care

I have always loved and been inspired by an account shared by Cecil Williams, who is now the pastor emeritus of Glide Memorial Church in San Francisco. When speaking at a transpersonal psychology conference in 1983, he shared his own story of an intense spiritual awakening as a young teenager. He suddenly began experiencing huge rushes of energy, along with visions of vast armies marching outside his windows and even across his bedroom. This went on for days, but his family was too poor to seek psychiatric help. Instead all the members of his extended family took turns sitting at his bedside, taking care of him until he came through the experience able to reenter normal life.

As he grew older, Williams was called to the ministry. As a pastor, he inspired and supported many people, even creating services to feed thousands of homeless people. His accomplishments in life have been vast and benefitted many. He has a truly remarkable legacy, and I believe this is partially because support, rather than psychiatric service, was available during a crucial transition in his life. A spiritual emergency can lead to a transformed and awakened life. We just need the right support to get through it.

I sometimes hear an awakening person say it is all about love. This view can help turn our life away from anxiety about, or fascination with, phenomena like visions and energy and unique powers. Adyashanti once said that when he began to teach he decided to do so from love alone. I have heard other teachers advise that, when you do not know what to do, ask "What would love do?" We can bring the power of love to awaken and heal into our life whenever we face a spiritual challenge, or even an ordinary life challenge. Love yourself and love the world, even while seeing the flaws. Then you will know you are in an astonishing emergence and not an emergency situation.

7. Ways to Support Ourselves and Others

Spiritual awakening brings us the realization that, as consciousness, we are one with a universal, timeless, eternal source. This is an invitation to feel blissfully alive and open to whatever life brings as we live in the moment. If there has been anything in your experiences of awakening, or in this book's descriptions of the challenges of awakening, that makes you feel hesitant to pursue and seek it, know this. The transition to living from your true nature may feel hard at times, but it holds the potential for extraordinary freedom and deep contentment.

Our journey brings challenges because it is a radical transformation. It is radical because it dissolves the false self, our conditioned sense of a separate "me," and because it changes how we relate to the world. We face unnecessary confusion along the way because spiritual awakening is not understood in Western cultures. We can be given mistaken spiritual advice by inexperienced friends and teachers—even within traditions that intentionally produce visions of alternate realities, journeys into the unknown, energy arousals, and shifts of consciousness. This happens because awakening is completely unique among each of us. So experiences can be discounted, dismissed, or misunderstood when they do not fit the belief system or direct experience of the teacher. Your teacher may not have experienced awakening or may have a very different way of engaging the process.

This chapter offers ways to support the awakening process so that it is grounded, peaceful, and centered. As you will see, we can support awakening by:

⊛ allowing change;

⊛ caring for our body throughout the process;

⊛ finding connections with a few people who are open to
our new perspective;

⊛ staying grounded in ordinary, earth-bound activities;

⊛ and seeing and releasing any fixed position of mind that
causes us to get stuck in either ego inflation or escaping
life.

The Basis of Supporting Awakening

We need two simple, basic things from others to support our transformation: listening and holding. We need someone's open attention
and presence through the challenges until we return to equilibrium.
This occurs only when there is a mutual agreement to trust the
process. Most of the time, this will not be available to us. We need
to care for ourselves. And as we learn to do that, we can turn to
others and be able to offer them the support they need. This will go
a long way toward curing the cultural deficiency for nurturing
unique awakening processes.

We can feel alone in our awakening, but actually we are not. We
are part of a web that has existed within all cultures for thousands of
years, woven by the people who set out on their journeys with the
same intention of awakening that is driving you. In all traditions,
they have encountered similarly disorienting experiences and realizations. Their awakenings infused more light and consciousness
into the collective mind. As an invisible, subtle energy, they are here
for you to offer a foundation of wisdom and love to hold your own
discovery.

We may sense their presence, and we may not until we deepen
our awakening. Many teachers recite their lineages to call upon its
presence, and beautiful Indian and Buddhist evocations have been
preserved for us through the centuries. The teachings of Jesus, such
as "The kingdom of God is within you," are part of this wisdom.
Many esoteric and mystery schools carry wisdom forward through

time that originated from people who began just like you, as spiritual seekers. When we are able to find a supportive spiritual community that works for us, where we feel safe and free to be honest, it can propel growth—as others support us and as we contribute support to others. If not, we can trust that we are already held in the web of a larger community that has been lighting the way all along, rooted in eternal wisdom and love.

EXERCISE: Ship Visualization

Early in my own awakening process, I dreamed I was on a pier and saw a miniature ship tipping over into the ocean, with many small people falling off into the water. I leaned over, righted the ship, picked up the people, and put them back on board. We all need to have an upright ship to navigate the waves of consciousness and support the various parts of ourselves on the journey.

Think of yourself as if you are on a ship. Consider what you need to keep your ship upright and sailing, ready for any conditions. Here are some things you may need:

- ✵ A captain to run things when the water is stormy
- ✵ A navigator to reassure you that the ship is headed in the right direction
- ✵ A crew to provide nurturing food and seasickness remedies
- ✵ A scholar to point out sites of interest along the way

When you have this kind of support, your journey of awakening will feel easier. Because even in the best of circumstances when other people care for you as you struggle, it is good to learn how to navigate the sea by yourself. It is your ship and your unique passage to liberation. Many of the answers you need are deep within your own heart. The reality is that your ship may sail through territory that teachers and guides are unfamiliar with.

Meeting the Needs of Transformation

Consciousness and energy brought us into a human form to have a life, and as we awaken they are laying the foundation for rebirth into new ways of living. Our exterior world may or may not change, depending on what it takes to align our authentic presence with the world. But our interior world is ready for transformation.

Our assumptions, habitual patterns, and preoccupations before awakening become irrelevant as awakening stabilizes into liberation. This is not a process of simple integration; it is transformation. Integration is rearranging our household to include new furniture. Transformation is moving to an unfamiliar country, leaving our language behind, and learning to live as part of a new culture. A sense of who we are is present, but the way we exist must change. It may not change the outward appearance of life, but awakening will restructure how we feel inside, how we experience life, and how we express in the world.

Even when we see the irrelevance of old patterns, they may arise again to create division within us or with others. We need to learn to face them with honesty and equanimity. This is a time of letting go. Trust the process. If possible, laugh at your foibles. Become curious about these life changes. And use the suggestions, exercises, and resources in this chapter to center yourself whenever, and however, it's needed. If you have moments of feeling overwhelmed or discouraged, here is an exercise that can help you gain some focus.

EXERCISE: Create Your Own Map

On a large piece of paper, draw a circle. Then create six pieces of the pie and label them with the following categories. These categories identify areas in which we all benefit from support.

Perspective

Physical Needs

Emotional Needs

Spiritual Needs

Creative Expression

Community

You can use each piece of the circle to identify, and write down, the essential ingredients that will bolster you. Look for ideas as you read through the rest of this chapter and add them to your circle. Brainstorm and add your own intuitions. As you gather ideas and notice what makes you feel centered and grounded in your daily life, this circle can become a map for drawing on sources of support when you need them.

Gain Perspective and Context

Many of us who seek awakening and enlightenment do not fully realize what experiencing transformation means, have misconceptions about it, and may secretly believe we are not capable of it. It's essential to gain perspective and context for our experiences, as awakening is natural to all humans when we are ripe for it. The mysterious events we may be coping with alone happen to many people who purposely, or accidentally, open to spiritual potential. We are not alone.

The first question most of us ask is: "What is happening and why?" If you are in a community that has no answer, or offers a negative interpretation of your experiences, don't be discouraged. Seek guidance elsewhere. Even Eckhart Tolle, now a respected spiritual teacher, asked this question. He sought an answer through extensive research into esoteric topics. As he found, ancient yogic and Buddhist scriptures describe awakening experiences that have been known for thousands of years to be natural within the context of spiritual practices. And there are many modern non-dual, Sufi, Buddhist, Advaita Vedanta, and Christian authors who offer insights that may inspire your journey even if they cannot address your specific upheaval and challenges. Some reading recommendations are offered in the Resources section. Here are some tips for increasing your understanding.

Identify What to Avoid

We can assist our process by avoiding certain ideas, places, and influences. By saying no to toxic patterns and interactions, both external and internal, we can keep our perspective clear.

- Don't go to places that make you feel exhausted or overly stimulated.

- Don't expose yourself to unhealthy environments, and if you are highly sensitive and tend to pick up the pain of others, avoid places and people where this is likely to happen.

- Don't hold on to a belief that there is something wrong with you.

- Don't chase the thought that you do not deserve freedom.

- Don't listen to people who believe in devils, invasive forces, or focus on battling darkness.

- Don't use food, drink, or substances that have a negative impact on your energy.

- Don't overdo practices using energy, breath, concentration, or altered states like channeling and visualization if they cause you discomfort or exhaustion.

You may find your sensitivity to places and people passes in time, so that you will be more comfortable in difficult environments that may have troubled you earlier in the process. Some people feel very at peace working in hospice, hospitals, social service settings, and even prisons once awakening has stabilized.

Focus On What You Seek

Focus your energies on opening to love and light. This is not a denial of the darkness we all face. Rather it is a recognition that darkness is part of the dance of phenomena, of opposites, but not an optimal place to dwell. Darkness can consist of mistaken and distorted interpretations of spirituality. So focus on the clarity, love, peace, freedom, and wisdom that you seek.

Simplify the Journey

When it comes down to it, the spiritual journey is about discovering the truth of who we are. Our interior world and lived experiences have little to do with traditional or mainstream views of spirituality and much more to do with the way we tune in to our inner spirit, our aliveness, and our perception. These changes may not be "spiritual" at all. If the journey becomes more about discovering truth and its evolution within us, we can feel more comfortable and freer from the burden of expectations. Consider how your process simply consists of changes in how energy and consciousness work in your body-mind to help you let go of the past and enjoy the moment that is happening now.

Transform Fear into Curiosity

Fear amplifies challenges. It triggers adrenalin, tightens the body, and blocks the free flow of life force. Like any other emotion, we must meet it. See it as an energy, similar to excitement, that is fueled by a thought.

Ask yourself what thought in your head supports fear, and you will begin to see how a simple thought can be its source. You may think "I must be crazy" or "Evil is present" or "What will my partner think?" or "This will never stop!" But a thought is only neurons firing, and it does not need to be believed or even evaluated. Too often we chew on certain thoughts as if they were important, when actually they are emotionally destructive. It isn't helpful to run from fear, so turn and face it with this exercise.

EXERCISE: Meeting Fear

At the first moment when you notice fear arising, ask yourself two questions:

- What part of me is noticing this fear?
- What thoughts are arising to support it?

Then breathe into your abdomen so that it rises on inhalation, and focus on the following.

- Ask the energy to calm down. You can imagine a color that feels soothing and penetrates the energy.
- See if you can use pure awareness to see the energy separate from the thought.
- If it is the energy itself you are afraid of, then ask it to go easy on you.
- Give your mind a positive thought from present-moment awareness, such as "You are really okay" or "This is just a curious event. If I feel like it, I might research it later."

Transform Resistance into Willingness to Wake Up

It is natural to feel resistance at times, especially if you are experiencing energies or mental distractions that are impinging on your work, relationships, and enjoyment of life. This is particularly difficult if you entered these experiences accidentally, without a spiritual intention. Many of us get stuck in phenomena, so that our energies are moving but awareness has not yet stabilized into realization. We can stay in the struggle indefinitely. *The most important thing anyone can do in this process is to keep going and thoroughly wake up.*

We are not the phenomena of the body-mind—it is a temporary vehicle. We are simply aware and conscious of it. This understanding is useless as a thought, as we must have a direct experience of it. We cannot force liberation, but we can be open and willing to receive it. Do more than surrender and let go. Look within yourself for what is already open and available to whatever life is offering. It may be a small opening at first, but it is within you, as the following meditative exercise can help you experience.

EXERCISE: Becoming Awareness

Sit in a comfortable chair where you will not be disturbed. Hold your back straight and relaxed, put your feet on the floor, and rest your hands on your lap.

For a few minutes, let your eyes take in the room where you sit, your ears acknowledge any sounds, your body feel the sensation of being held by the chair and the floor. You are aware of this present moment.

Close your eyes and bring awareness to your body. Become aware of any sensations happening internally: heat or coolness, vibration, a beating heart, tension, relaxation. You are aware of your internal world. If thoughts or feelings arise, awareness notices them and does not follow them. For a few minutes, be aware of how the breath moves in and through the body, supporting your existence.

Become curious about this awareness. It is an expansive quality that can move both inside and outside the body, even take in both worlds simultaneously. Is there any boundary to the sensation of being awareness?

Turn the awareness into itself. What is it? Feel awareness in the entire field of your body. Thinking about it is limited. Awareness can only be sensed and known.

Become this awareness without any object. Rest as this for as long as you wish.

When you are ready to return, gently reorient yourself to the chair and slowly open your eyes, noticing how awareness is looking out at the world or hearing any sounds. Sit in this sense of presence until you feel grounded where you are and ready to continue your day.

Ways to Cultivate Perspective

Beyond a deep and fearless inquiry into what is here, now, we can understand the nature and potential of awakening through the wisdom and expressions of those who have gone before us. The ecstatic poetry of Rumi, the angst of John of the Cross, and the images of Ten Oxherding Pictures from Zen offer insights into the challenges and process of realization, as well as ways to live as awakened people. There are so many ways you can shift in the moment toward an awakened perspective. Here are some you can try.

⊛ Find a role model or teacher who embodies what you seek, who you can study with, read books by, or listen to in person or through recorded talks.

⊛ Identify what you need to know, through intuition, and do research. Follow the threads of insight that feel most inspiring to you.

⊛ Write your questions on a piece of paper and leave them open until the answers come. When a question arises, there is usually also an answer deep within you that may surface when you least expect it.

⊛ When you have arguments and divisions in your mind, imagine taking a backward step out of thought. Be present with what is around you: the sight and sounds, air, and especially the beauty. Awareness is always right here and now. It never leaves you—you just become distracted.

⊛ Take a few deep breaths and, with each exhalation, focus energy below your neck to relax your body. Then bring your awareness into your heart area and feel how comforting inner silence can be.

⊛ Imagine you are a pine tree, or stand in yoga's tree pose with feet shoulder-width apart and hands joined in prayer position above your head. Feel flooded from above with peace, radiance, or stillness that goes all the way through your body and into your roots in the ground.

⊕ Pick a calming word or phrase to repeat, such as "love," "relax," or "here now," and imagine it flowing down into your entire body.

⊕ Sit with eyes closed for a while. Nothing is happening but being in this place, in this moment of now. Then open your eyes slowly, letting awareness look out of your eyes instead of being entangled in your thoughts.

⊕ Take time each day to feel gratitude for the blessings of your life.

Embrace Physicality

True support for awakening requires us to support our body. This book offers a lot of information about invisible energy flow and the subtle flow of consciousness. But there is also the organic, physical form of a body that we live within. This is our vehicle, something we need to have a life. To lead a full life, we need to take excellent care of our body—even with a spiritual, rather than material, view of the cosmos.

During awakening, almost anything can happen physically, as I described in chapter 5. This can feel challenging, especially if we have exhausted and overwhelmed our nervous system. The energies of transformation can bring puzzling sensations, including feeling:

⊕ Sweet *amrita* (nectar) flowing down your throat

⊕ Heat rising on one side of your body

⊕ Rolling heat and uncomfortable twinges in your back

⊕ Twisting motions in your neck

⊕ That you are floating a few feet out of your body

⊛ Inability to eat what you used to love

⊛ Sleeplessness

No matter what happens, the biggest mistake we can make is to ignore our physical needs. On the way to spiritual freedom, we can have insights into the illusion of the physical world and our body. Because physicality can seem fleeting compared to eternal, universal truths, we think it is trivial. We ignore the cues of sensations—whether of pain, hunger, or tiredness—to our detriment. The story of the Buddha demonstrates the ineffectiveness of going to extremes, as he went through periods of extreme indulgence and extreme deprivation in his own spiritual search, and eventually concluded he needed to find a middle way.[50] Since many spiritual teachings emphasize that we are not our body, seekers can go to the extreme of ignoring basic needs. We may overstress our nervous system with addiction to intense practices, or live in unhealthy conditions.

> Karen lived in India under the guidance of a guru who persuaded her to live in a forest, in a hut she built herself, and forage or grow her own food. Each day she did many hours of intensive breathing and meditation practices. She became weak and ill, as well as mentally disoriented, and returned home to the US needing medical and psychological care.

To function in our lives in the world, and to experience stability as we awaken, we need to appreciate form as much as emptiness. Our body and human environment are expressions of the one, infinite source. When we awaken to being pure awareness or consciousness, the next step is to see that all life as we see it (form) can only exist as expressions, or appearances, of this oneness. Therefore, physical existence deserves respect. As one teaching puts it, either everything is God or nothing is. Awake consciousness sees all as the dance of the one.

It is true that in order to know this essence we release attachment to form, but this is where the misunderstanding begins. We can release identification and attachment without giving up the basic value of having a body, a life, and people we love. When we give up unhealthy food addiction, we do not stop nourishing our body. Doing so would lead to illness. Similarly, we all give up our identification with being a child, but this does not mean we insist on removing play and fun from our life.

Attachment is an interior process of the ego. It occurs because we think something external is important to our self-image or to our happiness. When we awaken, these attachments naturally fall away because we have seen that the ego does not have a substantial purpose. We realize that happiness is an internal place rather than the result of material gain, and love is unconditional rather than dependent on reciprocity.

When we shed attachment to the body only to become attached to ethereal, formless spaces, we deny the value of the relative world and its relationships. We will not embody the wisdom and beauty we touch in awakening. We will not have physical strength for meeting the challenges that arise. We will not reach completion, living in the world with peace, contentment, and activity that is right for us.

We need to exist between two worlds—form and emptiness—so that they are one. If we are free in the emptiness of oneness, and deny the relative dance of forms through embodiment, we are not yet fully free. We need to take care of our body. Here are some ways to do that.

See Medical Practitioners

When having serious pain and physical limitations, always get a medical checkup. Being in an awakening process does not mean we cannot fall ill. Pains in the chest may very well be a heart problem and issues with cognition could indeed be a brain tumor. Awakening will not cause these things, but it doesn't prevent them either. Kundalini energy should not cause serious or persistent physical pain. As I discussed in earlier chapters, the intensity of energy arising can cause hormonal imbalances, put stress on vulnerable areas of the body, or bring a latent illness to the surface. They can also happen when we are so absorbed in spiritual practice that we disengage with our body's needs or try to energetically leave physicality behind. Do not assume a serious symptom is related to your spiritual practice until you have ruled out medical explanations. Some examples of medical causes for symptoms include:

- A foggy mind, depression, and exhaustion can be symptoms of a thyroid problem or vitamins B_{12} and D deficiencies.

- Flashing lights in the eyes can be a symptom of a detached retina or migraines.

- Inner sounds can indicate an ear infection or tinnitus.

- A continually shaking head can be related to TMJ, other jaw issues, or neurological issues.

- Abdominal or stomach pain, frequent indigestion, and severe cramping can have many serious causes that need medical treatment.

- Irregular heartbeat or chest pain can be the results of an array of cardiological problems.

See the appropriate doctor. Sometimes working with a naturopathic or osteopathic physician who tests for vitamin or mineral levels, allergies, and hormonal issues can lead to great solutions. Ayurveda and Chinese medicine practitioners can also distinguish between energy symptoms and illness. It may be that your diet is lacking an essential nutrient, your vision needs some correction, or your hearing needs an aid.

Come Home to Your Body

When we meditate, fall into an expanded state of consciousness, or have a profound opening experience, we can feel as if our body falls away. With some spiritual practices, it can be easy to feel disembodied. And it's extremely common for people with histories of physical or sexual abuse to protect themselves by leaving the body, a tendency that can begin at a very early age. It is a defense against feeling what is happening when it's too painful.

When we become disembodied, we can feel floaty, spacey, even unable to function in the world. It is hard to focus on conversations or tasks because our attention drifts. Our senses are less reliable so we may stumble, fail to hear someone, not notice we are hungry, and not be aware of what we need. This is why it's essential to learn how to come home to our body.

Knowing how to deliberately return our awareness to form and physicality benefits everyone. Counseling and body therapy can help us gradually recover a sense of being at home in our body. Grounding practices like the ones in this chapter can help us, on a day-to-day basis, remember to stay connected.

Use Body Awareness to Transition

We can sometimes feel disoriented because we move too quickly out of meditation or movement practice into regular, daily activity. When we rush from one state of consciousness into another, it is like moving unprepared from a heated room into icy weather. If our body can't adjust, we can become ill. Spiritual seekers benefit greatly from learning to move gently between worlds.

When you stand up from meditation, take a few minutes to be present before you move forward. Look down. Feel the earth below your feet. Enjoy the sensation of touching your feet to the floor. Be present with what is around you.

We can bring body awareness to daily activity for even more stabilization. Too often we are inclined to move with our head forward, rushing into life with mind first. I've been told that dancers are taught to move from their bellies, just below the naval. This gives them stamina and balance, and is also a good practice to help us live in our body. The Japanese word for belly, *hara*, is often referred to as a centering point. When we learn to focus on the belly, to feel the sensation of balance in this center point of our physical self, we can learn to bring the peace of meditation and stillness into daily life.

EXERCISE: Ways to Embody

Here are ways to connect consciousness with physical form. They can be done anytime, anyplace, whether we are returning from meditation and want to transition, waking from sleep, or recovering from an emotional shock. It doesn't take much for consciousness to feel connected and settled inside our skin.

- Feel your feet connected to the floor, sidewalk, or grass.

- Feel the sensation of air caressing your skin.

- Upon waking, lay or sit in bed and feel the sensations in your entire body before standing up.

- Try yoga stretches and gentle qigong movements that focus on grounding.

- When returning from meditation, use touch to notice the barrier between your form and the cushion or chair.

- Create a walking awareness meditation practice to feel more connected to your body and your environment.

- Feel what is going on inside your body:

  Do you feel warm or cool inside?

  Do you feel light or heavy?

  Where do you feel energy?

  Where do you feel space?

- Intentionally direct your awareness down from your head, through the neck, into the chest, belly, and legs.

- Pay attention to your stomach expanding as you inhale and relaxing as you exhale.

⊕ When you open your eyes from meditation or sleep, take a long time to look around the room and orient yourself.

⊕ Be aware of, and connect with, external sounds.

⊕ Do something quiet before you move into the tasks ahead of you, such as having a soothing cup of tea or enjoying nature through a window.

When Energy Overwhelms

When we struggle with overwhelming energy bouncing around us, or vibrating like a truck inside of us, the subtle energy field needs attention. The energy we are experiencing has two functions: the first is to clear away what is not needed and the second is to bring in new potentials. There are some common blockages that need to be cleared and then transformed as we awaken. They include:

Toxic events and experiences

Toxic people who may, or may not, still be in our life

Enduring grief over losses

Attachment to anything that we fear losing, but would be better off letting go

Toxic substances, such as drugs, cigarettes, or unhealthy food

Ways we learned to constrict our body rigidly in childhood as forms of defense

Old contractions of pain and suffering are trying to leave our body. Energy is trying to release their burden. If all these conditions were gone, imagine the openness and stillness we might experience. Imagine how we might see the world in a new way. We cannot force ourselves to let go, but we can allow energy to move. Are you willing to let go of the past?

We can support these functions by giving up being fearful of the energetic process and allowing it to be. Do not amplify it, but do not resist it. Learn to intuitively recognize when energy gets tense or constricted, and needs to release or relax. As we cooperate with energy, it will cooperate with us by being less invasive at times when we are in public, when we need to appear normal, and when we have had enough. You can build a relationship with this part of yourself.

EXERCISE: Ways to Calm Energy

If you feel overwhelmed by too much energy, it may be time to let go of all spiritual practices and rest. Listen to your body and intuition before engaging any practice, because not all can offer what you need and some may make challenges worse. Here are some resources that calm energy so you can relax, and therefore open, into awakening.

- ⊕ Meditation can help you embody, relax, and allow energy to move—I recommend the True Meditation practice, taught by Adyashanti, as a great way to begin.[51]

- ⊕ An Ayurvedic consultation can be helpful, as Indian medicine balances energy and practitioners evaluate imbalances to correct them with diet and herbs.

- ⊕ Chinese medicine doctors also address energy issues by balancing chi.

- ⊕ Gentle body therapies can soothe and ground you, such as cranialsacral therapy or acupressure, which is similar to acupuncture but more gentle.

- ⊕ Soothing yoga routines, rather than activating ones, can help.

- ⊕ Gentle qigong can help you move in a way that relaxes and opens the body.

- ⊕ Aikido is a martial art form that is also very good for loosening physical and psychological constriction.

- ⊕ Dance and song can be good releases, and you can choose the tempo, rhythm, lyrics, or genre.

EXERCISE: Harmonizing Energy Meditation

When energy feels too intense, or is stuck in one chakra area, you can harmonize it with this meditation. But it is a powerful practice, so only do it once a day. If this meditation or any other overcharges you, stop doing it and let it go. You are the one to decide what works for you.

Sit in a comfortable chair, feel your feet on the ground, your hands in your lap, and your body on the chair. Have your palms either up or down, whatever is most comfortable.

Become present and aware of the here and now of your location and body. Look around the room. Take a few deep breaths and as you exhale feel the connection your body has with the floor and the earth beneath it. Feel your arms touching whatever they are resting on. Be aware of what is in this moment in time, including:

The clothes touching your body and the air on your skin

Any sounds outside, letting them flow past in the background

The slight movements of your body as you breathe

Follow and count your breathing for ten breaths. Notice the air as it moves in and out of your nostrils. Then move awareness internally and scan your body to see what sensations are arising and falling away. Don't try to change anything, just include it.

Bring awareness to the base of your spine. Imagine a thin string of light moving from the center of the base and up the spine. It is soft and fluid and gentle. It moves up as you inhale and down as you exhale.

If you wish, imagine this string becoming wider so that it is the size of a thread, or a transparent tube, until it is wide enough that energy movement feels comfortable and happens with ease. You may feel a slight bliss or tingling in the body. If energy is in the head, you can imagine it moving down this tube into the heart or belly. Notice that energy follows your attention. If your head is uncomfortable, move the energy below the neck or somewhere that feels right for you.

Notice awareness simply observing this energy. Turn attention to the awareness itself. Begin to wonder at the presence that is simply here, observing all the aspects of your inner body and outer world. Sit for a short time (however long you wish) in this relaxation.

To end the session, come back to sensing your body in the chair and your feet on the floor. Open your eyes gently and softly, noticing how awareness looks around the room. Allow yourself to relax completely as you sit there with eyes open. Ask how your body wants to move before jumping to your thoughts for guidance. Stand up and do whatever you wish to do with your day.

EXERCISE: Harmonize Energy Through Sacred Sound

A classic kundalini yoga technique for relaxing and opening chakras, and moving energy up and down the spine, is chanting the *bij mantras*. These are sounds that resonate with different chakra areas. They are toned in a way that seems to vibrate each area, from the base of the spine to the third eye. As the third eye (ajna chakra) opens, the tone can move up through the head. Variations of this practice may be found on YouTube or in different schools of yoga, and you can even use the musical scale with them. It might be helpful to refer to the descriptions of the chakras in chapter 2.

Sound out the vibration of the area in your body-mind that you are focusing on opening or harmonizing. If you wish to release a block in one area, sit quietly for a few minutes, take a deep breath, and then make the sound for that area. Reserve some breath for the *m* sound at the end.

Chakra Name	Chakra Information	Number	Location	Bij Mantra Sound
Mooladhara	Foundation chakra	First	Base of spine	*Laum*
Swadhisthana	Dwelling place	Second	Genital area	*Vaum*
Manipura	Jeweled lotus, city of jewels	Third	Solar plexus	*Rahm*
Anahata	Unstruck, unbeaten	Fourth	Heart center	*Yaum*
Vishuddha	Purification	Fifth	Throat	*Haum*
Ajna	Command center, guru center	Sixth	Third eye	*Ohm*

Only make each sound two or three times to avoid overcharging the chakra. After voicing, you can simply be quiet and feel the sound within.

Remember that any energy practice can make your energy release more intense. Experiment, and if it evokes more of a rush than you are prepared to live with, then stop the practice. Have a soothing cup of tea or do one of the many grounding practices described later in this chapter.

Letting Energy Release

Although you may prefer to calm energy when it is too intense, sometimes it is impossible for any practice to do this. There are times when we must give it time to release in its own way. When kundalini phenomena arise strongly, all we can do is trust that the unfamiliar event is occurring to release a stressor, a suppressed memory, or a belief system that no longer serves us. We need to cooperate by giving ourselves time to let it flow. Then the energy can calm on its own, until the next episode. This tends to happen primarily in the early stages of the awakening process, and later when there is consistent stress that our body keeps trying to unload.

EXERCISE: Letting It Go

If energy is pushing up or down in your body, lie on your bed and let your body shake it out. Your body may bounce around or go into strange contortions like back bends or hand movements. Breathe into it. Let it move as it seems inclined to move. Try to keep your mind open and relaxed, just allowing things to be as they are. You can imagine being surrounded by light. If you feel connected to a spiritual entity or teacher, imagine he or she is standing by to protect you. Usually the body will shake and release for no more than fifteen minutes, but it can feel longer. There may be a sensation of peace when it stops, or consciousness may feel lifted into another dimension. It can also be tiring.

EXERCISE: Asking Energy to Wait

If your energy starts to move at inconvenient times such as while driving, teaching a class, or when you are somewhere impossible to be alone, then talk to it. In many cases energy will calm if you ask it to leave you for now. Set a time for when you will be at home and can let it release.

Find the Natural State Through Grounding

There are so many references to grounding in this book because it's a vital aspect of living in the world during a transformative process. Since consciousness can become fluid and less preoccupied with controlling your personal life, you may experience periods of feeling unfocused, disoriented, physically out of balance, and a need to bring your spirit back to earth. Most people feel this when coming out of long meditation retreats. They need to transition gently back into their worldly tasks and concerns.

When we are awakened, our natural state is to be fully present in the moment without being distracted by thoughts related to past or future. This is not to say that we never think about past or future, rather that unconscious demands, judgments, and rejections—even thought and ongoing mental chatter—don't seem important. When our focus is elsewhere, these things fade away, like a radio in a distant room. Sometimes they turn off for long periods of time.

We can learn to calm a busy thought process, or simply let go of attachment to it, by bringing our attention to what is happening this moment. This supports the opening and emergence of deep intuition. When we rest in this natural state, listen to it, and stay open to it, our true nature emerges to suggest new ways for resolving challenges.

When we are not grounded—balanced physically and emotionally in this natural state—the awakening process can be truncated. We end up in an unfocused, out-of-body, detached state. This state is not liberation; it is a hazy, partial samadhi that we can drift in for a while. But at some point we realize that, not only are we unable to function effectively, we also need to embody our realization to keep awakening. It is time to come back to earth.

Just as we rise to reach toward spirit, we can also bring spirit down to earth and ground it. We need to create a bridge between the spiritual and earthly, the profound and mundane, the transcendent and relative aspects of life. We do this by connecting our body with the earth and everyday human activities. Here are some physical ways that help us make this connection. These suggestions came from clients who found something that worked. Perhaps you will add to the list.

- Walk in nature, focusing on the feel of your feet on the ground.

- Breathe in the word *here* and breathe out the word *now*.

- Lean against a tree to feel an intimate connection with nature.

- Lie down on the grass and energetically sink into it.

- Dance outdoors, on the earth, or indoors to drumming music.

- Express what you feel through creative activities like painting, writing poetry, playing an instrument, singing, and moving.

- Play with pets or young children.

- Garden and dig in the dirt to seed and nurture plants.

- Bake bread, kneading it the old-fashioned way.

- Work with clay.

- Move from your belly, your center of gravity, as you walk or hike.

- Try drinking burdock tea or warm milk with sugar and melted ghee in it.

⊛ Eat root vegetables and protein.

⊛ Get a massage and stay awake through it.

Direct Your Mind into Your Body

A simple way to move energy is to bring attention from our busy mind gradually down through the neck and chest, into our belly. Putting awareness any place below the neck is a quick way of coming back into the ordinary and earthly world, quieting thoughts, and bringing overly active energy to a place in the body that is quieter and slower. Since we spend so much time thinking, worrying, getting information from smartphones, reading, problem solving, listening, and seeing, our brain gets overloaded. Consciously bringing attention down, into the chest or the belly, can be very soothing. Even awareness in the hands and feet can help. If you are in sitting meditation, feel your sitz bones against the cushion or chair. When you lie down, feel your body connected to the bed or the floor. Feel how one set of molecules (the bed) is supporting another (you). Relax and sink in.

Balance the Lower Chakras

Some meditations focus on the third eye, or ajna, chakra just above and between the eyebrows. While this may produce awakening phenomena, it can cause disorientation in the ordinary world. Focusing on this part of the body may produce headaches, itching, dizziness, or floating sensations. We can be so eager to raise energy, transcend suffering, and expand our mind and spirit that we ignore the lower chakras. Even when our heart is open, the lower chakras must also be balanced or survival needs, sexuality, desire, and mood can become difficult to manage.

Some people find it easy to move into altered and expanded states of consciousness, have out-of-body experiences, and receive spontaneous or sudden awakenings. But they develop physical illnesses or disorientation. We can detach from feelings in the lower body, especially with a history of physical or sexual abuse, and therefore lose our ability to ground energy in our body. This may happen because kundalini was disturbed or aroused by abuse, we had difficult birthing or near-death experiences, or an accident jolted the base of our spine. Alternately, energy in the lower chakras can suddenly rise and disturb us without traveling far enough to lead us into awakening because it cannot move into and beyond the heart. So it is important to tend to, and seek balance for, all the chakras.

EXERCISE: Tending to the Lower Chakras

Yoga postures, or asanas, do include helpful grounding practices, especially if done while focusing on breathing and moving energy. Here are some simple movements to ground energy through the first three chakras.

Mooladhara, Root Chakra: Sit cross-legged, holding your ankles lightly. Contract the muscles of the anus and perineum, pulling upward slightly. Inhale slowly as you rock forward and pull on your hands. You are pressing the spine forward. Then release your feet down and exhale as you rock backwards. You are rocking forward and backward on the base of your spine, while feeling the sensations there.

Swadhisthana, Second Chakra: Sit cross-legged or in a chair and relax your hands on your knees. Put attention on the chakra, located behind the genitals. Rotate your body in a circular motion from the naval. Then relax and be attentive to your breath and genital area.

Manipura, Third Chakra: Lie on your back and put your hands under your hips. Raise the right leg up 90 degrees on the inhalation and release it down on the exhalation. One minute with the right leg and one minute with the left leg. Relax. Then raise both legs together. Inhale up. Exhale down. Keep awareness on the third chakra area, located a few inches below the naval.

Additional Grounding Practices

You can find exercises for grounding on YouTube or through a yoga or qigong teacher. Some practices may activate more energy than you want, while others help the body to open, relax, and harmonize. You may need to experiment to find what feels best for your unique body and energy system. Do not push yourself beyond what's comfortable, and carefully assess each practice to be sure it's working for you and not overstimulating your system. Among the many qigong practices for grounding energy, I especially like this one.

EXERCISE: Qigong for Grounding

Stand with feet slightly apart and knees slightly bent. Swing your arms from left to right across the body, then back again from right to left. Swing far enough that the left hand gently slaps your right hip and, on the return, the right hand gently slaps the left hip. Keep awareness on the feet and relax into the movement.

Facing Psychological Issues

A lot of change happens to spiritual seekers engaging an awakening process. From a psychological perspective, change is about letting beliefs and attachments fall away so that the drive and demands of ego fade. Then we become more closely aligned with our intuitive, inner truth.

This is very different from self-improvement. Many of us have sought growth and contentment through various therapies that help us uncover old issues, become healed from childhood loss or trauma, and individuate—learning to more fully express who we are. As part of this journey toward healing, we have learned to dive deeply into our past and to fully express our emotions. We can be grateful for these changes, which do enrich our life. But a spiritual awakening requires a different kind of inquiry not so involved in our mind's perspective on how we can improve. Instead of simply seeking happiness, we question our existence as a separate self that lives and dies in one brief life, and explore how we are more. We seek deeper truths that underlie our sense of self because we want something that is not so transient, that is free and unified. We are not improving our self; we are looking past the one who feels it needs improvement.

Even though we are on a fundamentally different journey, psychological issues do still arise. Self-judgment, inflation, and emotional reactivity will come up. While traditional therapies are related to behavior change, changing thoughts, or intellectual analysis, some techniques such as EMDR, somatics, Hakomi Method, Focusing, and guided imagery can be helpful because they use presence and awareness to support clearing. Here are the two primary ways psychological work can assist the awakening process.

Resolving Unfinished Psychological Business

If you have not engaged with therapy much and if you have encountered trauma in your life, you are likely to find old memories, wounds, and conflicts coming up either in meditation or during energy releases. If you are hurting and unable to release painful stories from your past, then seek a therapist specializing in the issues you want to resolve. If you have conflicts with a partner, child, or family member that you need to resolve because they continually trigger your old reactive patterns, see a relationship counselor and find resolution.

Learning to Be Okay with Uncertainty

When awareness moves beyond the boundaries of the personal, panic may follow. Our mind fears losing its familiar hold on life. The feeling of losing control can trigger physical and emotional symptoms, generate nightmares, and cause the mind to race into catastrophic thinking. When our sense of identity feels unstable, we can fear we are mentally ill. All of these emotions disrupt the awakening process. Traditional therapy is not useful for this issue because most therapists are trained to strengthen personal identity. But if you can find a therapist with an understanding of spiritual emergence, perhaps through one of the networks I suggest in the Resources section, he or she can help calm fears, uncover old experiences that may be getting in your way, suggest practices to be more present, and offer tools for calming anxiety.

Ways to Facilitate Psychological Change

Spiritual practices will not help you leapfrog over the past. Instead, they force you to face the impacts of these events. The process reveals your conditioned attitudes and the reactions that result from them so you can release them. Spiritual awakening is about freedom from personal history. Here are some ways to move in that direction.

Become Aware of Awareness

Whatever arises in you is noticed because of awareness. This awareness is a neutral witness to all your thoughts, emotions, reactions, and experiences. It is an aspect of consciousness that is always present before the arising of a thought, feeling, or sensation. To facilitate your psychological awakening process, get curious about this awareness. See if you can become aware of awareness. What is aware of you? Where is it rooted? Is that what you are? By learning to access awareness in peaceful moments, you can remember to be aware in troubling moments also. Knowing ourselves as awareness leads to waking up. When we fully awaken, most of our patterns, moods, and energetic problems improve greatly.

EXERCISE: Meeting Your Truth

When you feel caught by an emotion you can't release, like fear, longing, rage, or grief, set aside time to face it. Be sure you will not be disturbed and sit down as if to meditate. Take a few breaths. As you breathe in, feel the sensation of this emotion. As you breathe out, imagine the emotion dissipating into space.

When you are ready, accept that you have this difficult feeling. Be aware of how it feels and where you feel it in your body. Enter the heart of the emotion. See if there is a story attached or beliefs clinging to it.

Imagine you can go beneath the surface of this feeling by opening a door behind or underneath it. As you open this door, you may see another feeling or picture or assumption. Sit for a while with what arises. Then open the door behind this. Keep opening doors and inquiring, sitting with each picture or feeling.

You will likely reach a state in which a truth arises that shifts your relationship to the problem. This last, revealing insight breaks the power the emotion has held over you. You may discover a truth that transforms.

Sometimes you may need to repeat this exercise more than once, whenever the old emotion reasserts itself in response to some event or experience. Keep going, all the way through the feeling, until you return to the presence of aware consciousness. In time you will become free from this reactivity.

Heal Through Art

Awakening needs expression. Many spiritual seekers have found outlets for what feels inexpressible in their lives through painting, writing, music, dance, songwriting, and other creative activities that move them. Great artists throughout history express the joys of awakening in their work, and I encourage you to turn to them for inspiration, insight, and examples of what you can do with your own artistic interests. Here are some examples:

- *The Red Book* is the journal Carl Jung kept through an intense period of transformation, inner turmoil, and spiritual awakening. Journaling in words, pictures, or both can help release inner conflicts.

- Nicholas Roerich was a Russian explorer and artist whose soaring paintings of the Himalayas reveal radiant moments of awakening.[52]

⊛ Sacred music from around the world opens our hearts because the composers lived in a sacred world. Christian and Buddhist monks have recorded chants with the power to transport consciousness. Kirtan, the chanting in sacred Indian music, also does this.

⊛ The great Sufi poets Rumi and Hafiz expressed awakening in the vivid images and stirring feelings of their verses.

⊛ One full-time artist traveled around the world creating something of beauty wherever she stayed. Among many other things, she carved a goddess in an Indian cave, built a shrine in a Bhutanese forest, and designed a water tower for an African tribe.

EXERCISE: Creating a Mandala

Creating a mandala is a ritual and prayerful meditation. The mandala is a sacred symbol of wholeness used by monks in some Eastern traditions, and is created by many indigenous societies as a healing practice. The many symbols found in mandalas are intuitive expressions of wholeness that regenerate the spirit, explore the psyche, calm the mind, and express what we cannot put into words. They reveal unity between humanity and the cosmos, and making one brings us into relationship with our center. You may create one as a unique expression and then discover it is connected to universal experience.

Use a plate to trace a large circle in the center of a piece of paper. You can use white pencils on black paper, or white paper with colored pencils. Sit in meditation for a short time, inviting a sacred image to arise. When you are ready, draw whatever you wish, using rulers or tracing patterns, doing freehand drawing, balancing your images around the center of the circle. Let your intuition guide you, and do not demand perfection. This is for you to freely express.[53]

Witness Without Judgment

We can become a more open presence with more compassionate awareness for whatever is arising—without judgment. This is a big psychological shift that takes a lot of us by surprise. We can nurture this change by noticing our judgments, whether of ourselves or others, and not attaching importance to them. When we feel a flash of self-judgment, it may be an alert that we need to understand something about our self or our history. Sitting with it until we can see beneath the vivid emotions, storylines, or thoughts that prompted the judgment will help us discover our true nature. We all make errors in our lives. Once we are awake, we can sit with a disturbing fact about our self, or someone else, and simply stay with it. We can feel acceptance, curiosity, and love. The judgment may then diminish or dissolve into a sense of wholeness. Once we give up judging and condemning ourselves, we are able to disregard thoughtless judgments of others because we understand how confused a human mind can be.

EXERCISE: Releasing Judgment

When you are condemning someone, take time to make a list of all their failings. Then ask yourself what you have in common with this list, and why those tendencies provoked you to judge. Ask yourself these questions:

- What do I believe that makes me judge this action?
- Where does it come from in my conditioning?
- Am I willing to carry these difficult feelings with me, or would I rather be free?
- Is it my thoughts that are making me unhappy?
- Without thinking, can I simply feel this emotion?
- Do I need to carry this around in my brain, or can I put it down in the service of love?

Make Adjustments as You Go

Listen to your internal rhythms and make adjustments that work for the unique person you are and that are authentic to your deepest truths. Sometimes we may need more flexibility in our body, other times more openness of mind or heart. Sometimes we just need to relax and watch a movie. Other times we need to attend to the tasks of ordinary daily living, like cleaning the kitchen or getting to the gym. It is essential to become honest with our self about what we need to find balance in our life. Be authentic as you tune into the deepest sense of what is right for you. Be autonomous as you act to align your life with what you know.

Consider Your Diet and Health

To support your psyche, look at your diet to see if it can be improved. Avoid intoxicants, sugar, and other factors that can impact mood. Add enough protein and root vegetables to your diet, as they help with grounding. Supplements and teas can help your particular constitution find balance. Explore balancing your mind by balancing your diet with a naturopathic doctor, or through Ayurveda or Chinese medicine systems.

If you are overwhelmed by depression or dark moods and thoughts, get a medical exam or physical. Be sure your hormones are okay, that your nervous system is not damaged, and rule out any physical condition that may be affecting you.

Seek to Better Align Your Environment and Relationships

Look at your lifestyle. When we are awakening, we live less comfortably with a toxic relationship or environment. And we are less willing to carry as much stress as we once were. Some spiritual seekers believe that, if they are awake, they should be able to be happy anywhere. So they do nothing to change their relationships or environments for the better. As a result, they stay trapped in psychological patterns for a long time. Be honest in observing how you live your life, and listen to your intuition about changes that would serve you during this important time of transition.

Face Your Traumas and Your Emotions

With trauma as part of your history, face it as best you can and support the wounded part of you. You may be awakening into a larger, more universal awareness, but this does not mean you can abandon yourself as human, with human pains and memories. For recurring issues or patterns that are related to grief, anger, or depression, it helps to see a therapist.

When an uncomfortable mood arises over and over again, begin to chart it or journal about it. This can help you identify its triggers. Become curious about what happened earlier in the day, what you ate, who you talked to, what you were thinking about, and write them down. After doing this a few times, look to see if a pattern emerges. Once you know the trigger, you can see if you can avoid it or respond to it in a new way by dealing with what precedes it.

Qualities to Cultivate That Support Awakening

Those of us who long for God, truth, or liberation are driven by the most true and enlightened part of ourselves. Awakening is not a sideline activity, an accomplishment, something to cross off our bucket list, nor simply an adventure in consciousness. The enlightenment of our consciousness is freeing, but consciousness is so undemanding it allows any whim to distract us and never stands in the way. This is what makes awakening so elusive.

Enlightenment is a refined flower seeded in our heart that will only push through the surface when our heart is free of the weeds of distracted thoughts, harmful activities, and egoic assumptions about who we are. This doesn't mean we live in extreme states of self-denigration and self-denial. Instead we discover the simple joys of life. Almost any encounter, felt fully and experienced with innocent wonder, can open us to receive grace: the awesomeness of a sunset, the beauty of a baby, the soulful eyes of an animal. Life is full of opportunity to activate the spark of awakening.

These sparks can only stabilize into an enlightened life when we are real, honoring our deepest truth, and nakedly sincere with ourselves. If liberation is what we want more than anything, we will find the courage to keep our heart open, look deeply within, allow what isn't true to fall away, and relax into the core of beingness. These qualities support us along the way.

Equanimity Honors Life's Challenges

Our true nature has no resistance; argument and aversion belong to the mind. When events arise that need addressing, such as confusions we must clarify, dramas we must sort out, or messes we must clean up, we can meet them with equanimity. Life is not interfering with our spiritual development. It is asking for something from us. Rather than resist it, we must honor it, and authentic responses will arise naturally. Then we can move with the inevitable flow of challenges in life.

Openness Makes Us Honest

Before any growth can happen, we need to be open with ourselves. Then we can be honest and willing to face whatever arises. This fundamental state then opens us to new experiences, to making necessary changes, to finding our unique rhythm, and to living authentically.

Flexibility Helps Change Happen

Just as flexibility can be physically cultivated, it is as important to develop flexibility of mind and spirit. This helps us be willing to change, transform, and adapt to the ways that the journey is affecting us. In this transitional time, we can be curious about the anomalous events that arise, examine what they are telling us, and be willing to make lifestyle adjustments to align with these new insights. This may mean that we make small changes to support awakening, such as:

- Creating a less stressful work schedule

- Giving up alcohol and mind-altering substances

- Taking fewer classes, or more enjoyable ones

- Staying away from big-box stores

- Avoiding disturbing films and news programs

- Resolving interpersonal issues or taking time away from toxic relationships

- Taking time for a consistent meditation practice

- Finding a supportive community

As we discover that one way of living no longer works for us, our transformation and embodiment will happen more comfortably and more smoothly if we are flexible about how we live, and can make the needed changes.

Authenticity Supports the Process

When spiritual seekers are out of alignment with truth, we feel terrible. Most of us have old patterns that are self-serving or reactive. After a deep awakening that pattern becomes more uncomfortable. Sometimes we find our self following old, go-to choices because they have led our behavior for so long, and wish we had listened to the intuitive voice within that comes from our heart or gut to tell us to do something differently.

A time may come when we realize many beliefs and reactive patterns have dissolved. But some remain stubborn: belief systems we take for granted, feelings like inadequacy and self-doubt, resistance to certain people or concepts, judgments of others, even a style like irritability. These patterns are natural human tendencies, and may or may not resolve in this lifetime. Yet they do not reflect our true nature, which is at peace with itself and the world. Caught inside this paradox, we can feel bound by the habits of a separate self even as we feel it no longer exists. So we need to respond with authenticity. Rather than living from self-centered expectations of ego, we live from the values of our soul.

Authenticity Can Navigate the World

As I described in chapter 5, being awake in the world can at times bring up a challenging experience of alienation. Here again, we need to be authentic. With authenticity, we can be quiet and relaxed about our awakening experiences and discoveries. We can trust what we know without the need to push it on anyone else. We can offer pointers if someone asks, but this is not a spiritual belief or teaching to proselytize. Friends will notice and appreciate changes, but they don't need to understand just what happened to us.

As soon as experience becomes a story or a concept to be accepted by others, we know our separate self has appropriated it. We seek recognition, approval, and understanding from others because we are frightened or we doubt ourselves. But the fully awakened, true nature of the universe has no need to be understood. It is full within itself. We too can rest in this knowing, feel authentic, true to our awakening insights, and free from the need to convince others of anything.

Awakening Comes and Goes Along the Way to Embodiment

Even awakening at a deep level doesn't mark an end to the journey. Our patterns, impulses, and desires may fall away but most of us will occasionally feel their return. Many express this feeling as "I had it, then I lost it!" It can take a long time to live from awakened consciousness, so we must learn to navigate its ebbs and flows, its coming and going.

Authenticity helps, as listening to the quiet place within invites us to do what feels right, personally—despite many opinions from everyone else. Adyashanti has called this way of living "having allegiance to the soul." He points out that, instead of asking how we can be in an awakened state forever, we need to ask, "What does that revelation ask of me? How can I best serve it in my life?"[54]

These questions help us embody insights and realizations that impact our life so we can find our authentic direction. Answers reveal themselves as we release the influence of our past positions and stand open to this moment. To embody awakening, we must let go of personal demands and express the humility, love, and service that is awakened living. This requires courage and a heartfelt willingness to be true to our deepest understanding. Authenticity can become a deep and honorable ally at the core of our own being, who will help us find our way.

EXERCISE: The Authenticity Ally

You can visualize your authenticity as an ally walking next to you, holding a pole with a lantern dangling from it. He or she is lighting your way. The light may be feeble at first, it could at times burst into brilliant brightness, but either way it is helping you see how to navigate your life so that it is in alignment with awakening.

Return to the feeling of having an inner ally when you need to be patient with yourself or with your experience. Find strength in this ally, because he or she helps you live in a way that is true to your deepest wisdom. This is authenticity.

The Blessings of Awakening

We honor awakening by: taking care of us, trusting that our movement is a life-enhancing direction of human evolution, understanding the process, making adjustments so we become more open, and turning inward to seek truth as it moves through us.

Even if they seem fleeting, value the grace you have received, the insight you have gained, and the freedom you have earned. Appreciate the many strengths you are gaining as you navigate this journey. Take time to enjoy life and appreciate the beauty around you.

When we face and heal our own suffering, we break patterns in the family line so they don't extend to future generations. Trust the process so it can heal and diminish suffering in the world. Embrace the invitation to love unconditionally.

When the seeker or experiencer in us is no longer dominating our life, and challenges of adjustment are easing, we can ask our heart for our next authentic movement: "What wants to come through me?" Then we lean in to life with the openness and curiosity we have been nurturing all along. With humility, we act in authentic expressions of service that are unique.

This is how our need for support ceases, questioning ends, and we relax deeply into life. Does this mean the journey comes to an end? I once asked Adyashanti this question and he replied, "How can it ever end? We are talking about the infinite."

PART THREE

THE CONTINUAL UNFOLDING OF LIBERATION

8. Blissful Losses in Transformation

As we move through the awakening process, we experience many moments of letting go. Our emotional pains surface and we face them. We let go of what we no longer need and support our body as it adjusts to new sensations. There can be moments when we feel loss for our old life and exhaustion from the struggle. It can seem like as soon as we come to terms with one realization, we find ourselves adjusting to the effects of another.

Julianne felt fed up with the process. After thirty years of doing yogic and Buddhist practices, awakened or not, she wanted out. But there is no emergency exit. The only way out is forward. After a supportive talk with her teacher, a shift happened and her resistance fell away. Shortly afterward, she awoke in the middle of the night.

I woke up feeling so not there that I doubted I was physically alive. I checked to see if anything in my direct experience offered proof for my physical existence. I couldn't find it. Only knowing remained. My sleep was disrupted, as again and again when waking there was only the knowing and nothing known. The next day, while crossing a street in the evening, another shift happened. The car headlights looked very different, like they were dissolving. I thought, Oh no, not again. But I had to drive home so I refused to look more closely. At home, I took stock of what happened. And I saw it. Everything is one vibrational field. What I look at is me, looking at me. When I eat, it feels like eating myself. When walking, I walk through myself again. It is very tender, beautifully intimate. The best way to express it would be: everything is made from love. That evening, I felt drawn to listen to one of my favorite Bach cantatas. So much bliss arose that I completely dissolved into it. I felt wonderful, like being home again, and stayed in bliss for a long time. While dissolved into it, I saw that I have never been born.

When we fully let go into the experience of the moment, like Julianne we may fall into a new realization, closer to knowing inherent oneness. Openness facilitates release and we can intentionally open by taking time each day, through meditation or relaxation, to allow energy and consciousness to move as inclined. Whenever we release a physical blockage or an emotional contraction, as Julianne describes, we momentarily lose feelings of separateness and come closer to knowing freedom. Then we can relax into joy and peace.

Human change seems to involve loss. When we move from infancy to childhood we give up dependency and learn self-sufficiency. During adolescence we lose connections with childhood toys. As we move into marriage or partnership we exchange some of our independence to cultivate cooperation and sharing. When we are in an awakening process, we can expect old attachments and patterns to fall away. We lose the addiction to our former identity.

This is a release into life and love, not a descent into barrenness. It is the transformation from limitation, living in the shadow of who we could become, to the liberation of being aligned with the deepest longing of our soul: to know our true nature.

Loss of the Autobiographical Self

Tom Thompson, founder of The Awakened Heart Center for Conscious Living, has called this transformation "the loss of the autobiographical self." He first heard the concept from neuroscientist Antonio Damasio, who uses it to label an area of the brain that holds memories and future plans, and is responsible for a stable sense of self. Damasio says that other species do not have this autobiographical self, which develops social-cultural patterns and regulations.[55] Thompson's use of the phrase conveys the aspect of our mind that controls our sense of being a separate identity. This is what changes during a spiritual emergence.

The autobiographical self is what you think you are and, for the most part, what you experience reality to be. It is an ongoing story that you are always telling yourself in your mind. Almost all of your thinking is an internal dialogue oriented around "you," your autobiographical self, and its imagined life. It requires constant embellishment and propping up as it believes itself to be a noun, an actual entity, when in fact it is a verb, a flow of interpretive thought… Every "thing" is always changing, moving, shifting, appearing, and disappearing. In actuality, there are no nouns, only verbs. Sooner or later an autobiographical self notices that it, and everything else, has no solid or permanent reality.[56]

What Is Transformation?

Essentially, transformation dissolves the power and limitations of the autobiographical self. The stories and goals are not forgotten, but they become irrelevant. The sense of a separate "me" who is burdened by the past and driven into the future simply loses all steam. Thoughts concerned with appearances like accomplishments, accumulation, admiration, and expectations are seen as simply the autobiographical self, the story of a life. This is not just a psychological adjustment, it is an energy adjustment as well. The "working mind," which navigates the day-to-day details of our life, remains, without attachment to the personalizing tendency of the autobiographical mind.[57]

Losing a sense of self may sound like a big loss, but think about your life. Hasn't it happened already, over and over again? Is the person you believed you were at age twelve the same person you thought yourself to be when you were twenty? Were you the same at thirty or forty or fifty? Our body is continually dissolving and rebuilding, and so is our mind. Everything we learn, and all the new experiences we accumulate, change our inner landscape. This impacts our perceptions of self, our capacities, and our positions in the world. The autobiographical self of today is an image, just like all the past images were. As we awaken into liberation, the old images are harder to sustain, and we see a new dimension to what it means to be human.

Annette had a Christian background and began seeking awakening after her retirement. She practiced meditations she learned from books. In a ritual with a small group of friends, she slipped into an awakening that left her feeling both graced and stunned by a loss of self.

> I leaned back with arms wide. As my head touched a pillow, I was propelled into what seemed like a vast, empty universe. I thought, This must be what it's like to die and also I have been here before. I saw a small dot of light come from the left that melted into the emptiness. After that there was no thinking, just peace and quiet and nothingness. It was a sense of being one with all. The next day I picked up a spiritual book and read a description of my experience. I found myself in tears, feeling I had lost something, a view I previously held of the world, of myself. I had awakened out of my familiar sense of self into a much greater reality, something far beyond anything I knew existed.

Like Annette, many of us have moments that open us to trust and that transform our worldview. As the need to protect a self-image disappears, we can bring these insights into our lived experience by relaxing, opening, and exploring new capacities and potentials.

When transformation happens, it is not our doing. All we can do is allow it. Allowing feels hard for most of us because we firmly believe we need to stay in charge or nothing useful will happen. This is one reason liberation takes some time. Most of us need to let go in small steps, like children learning to step in water and eventually swim. We are adjusting to the new environment blossoming inside.

This new environment is *beingness*, as opposed to the *doingness* of the mind. We don't become passive or dull or disinterested in living. Instead, we feel deep intuition about each unique moment so we can follow what calls us. We feel peace and clarity of mind. Gradually we move closer to liberation.

Three Obstacles to Transformation

Awakening begins with slipping through portals that offer expanded moments of perception, which is often followed by the surfacing of unconscious material that can feel difficult to face. As we become more compassionately aware of our history, we heal and evolve. Three specific obstacles can put brakes on this process if ego takes hold of our spirituality.

Identifying with Spiritual Attainment

A spiritual ego can arise to help us escape from facing the clearing process. It can feel very painful to lose the fullness of an awakening event. When human foibles and emotions inevitably return, we can feel depressed or anxious. We may have expected to remain in a transcendent state and to give up ordinary life. We can cling to awakening glimpses and try to repeat them over and over, instead of allowing a natural evolution to occur. Or we can become fearful that we will return to the old identity we believed we had left behind.

Our ego can even appropriate the spiritual process, jump into inflation, and declare itself enlightened, which curtails any capacity to end separation and find stable realization. Naively assuming we are enlightened, and eagerly rushing forward to tell the world, is simply a re-identification with the sense of "I." It might give "me" a higher purpose, but it shuts down vulnerability. This can derail the awakening process and quickly get us over our head with friends and students. Remember that the "me" cannot get enlightened, because "me" is only a facade. It does not exist in the way the mind believes it does.[58]

Spiritual Ruts

We can fall into the ruts of stubborn attitudes, emotional patterns, or old beliefs that reignite and take a long time to dislodge. These may be related to fear, attachment to religious belief, a sense that we no longer fit into mainstream culture, or other unique issues.

We get stuck for so long because when we're attached to old patterns of being, shifting perspective can be very difficult. Awakening challenges everything we assume is true, especially existing as a separate "I," and that sense of "I" can rebel against awakening.

Attachment to Spiritual States

Unusual spiritual gifts can arise, which may become the foundation of a new identity. You might find greater synchronicity in your life, in which you have a thought and then its object instantly manifests. You may find yourself drawn to healing others or using a new psychic power. While these abilities can indeed be gifts that will become part of your life work, if ego attaches to these new experiences, deeper realization can halt. This tends to happen more when the gifts are used commercially or you gather followers attracted to your special skills.

Realizations Along the Way

There are states that invite us to see where we are still stuck in separation, personal identity, or ego's hold on spirituality. We may want to be recognized, feel arrogant, be reactive to criticism, or feel judgment toward someone. These are opportunities to face parts of our self that are asleep and need to be awakened. Then, as conditioned assumptions and impulses are seen to be illusions and released, we may feel purposeless. We might be frightened by emptiness.

Some therapists will be concerned if you report these conditions, because they are the opposite of mainstream ways of looking at building a healthy ego. Students in some of these stages have asked me "What is the point of living?" or "Am I losing my mind?" or "How can I function in the world?" But these are shifts in how we know our self and not the losses they seem to be. They are part of clearing, recognized for centuries in monastic traditions. Here are the predictable realizations likely to arise to help you release restrictions on your freedom.

Unknowability

This is an awareness of being unable to locate the "I." It is not the body, not the thoughts, not the feelings. If we look, we cannot find it. We suspect that it is a contrived sense holding together our history, experiences, and beliefs, that it is an illusion. Asking "Who am I?" thrusts you into the unknown.

Productive Doubts

Feeling doubt about, or loss of faith in, teachings and beliefs you formally embraced that framed your worldview—and losing all interest in rules, rituals, and dogma—can be painful. You may see that the beliefs are illusory, just products of mind and not essential to life or spiritual growth. When this happens, it's an invitation to go deeper into yourself to see how these beliefs have framed your sense of reality. Beliefs are not reality; they are thought forms. Reality is what is happening here and now.

Futility

Your desires may shift, whether for food or sex, certain habits or old friends, accumulation of power or wealth. You may witness your reactions and be disheartened by your behavior. The reactions may be based on desires to have your way or to be right. You realize that as soon as one desire is met another arises, so attachment to these experiences is futile. As soon as you meet one goal, you search for another, and may become bored with the first accomplishment. You will see the futility of many things as you awaken.

Shedding the Old

You may no longer care for the material things you have accumulated and feel like leaving it all behind to wander the world. Disinterest can spread to things you enjoyed in the past. A fogginess of mind can arise when trying to do tasks that require organized thinking, and you may fear losing the ability to function. The fogginess will pass, but this journey may completely restructure the way you live your life.

Spiritual Detachment

Your interest in transcendent spiritual practices or longing for mystical experience may fall away. If these were your main preoccupations, you may feel empty of all goals and not know what to do with your life. Adyashanti has said spiritual attachment is the last thing to go. If all your psychic energy has gone into focusing on acquiring mystical experience or becoming enlightened, it is a shock when this last desire collapses. If you have felt a need to leave a community, or you've been rejected from one that sustained you for years, you may feel rudderless in ordinary life. This is felt as loss, but is actually a liberation. You may benefit from taking another look at your beliefs and all you were trained to think about spirituality. Awakening is much bigger than any system that teaches it.

Restlessness

There may be a stage of restlessness because you no longer believe in an "I" who tells you how to live or what to do. You may feel you are living outside of time and space. If you feel lost in emptiness, and withdrawn from life, this restlessness may be your heart pushing you to discover a further step toward liberation: living it in the world. Follow your heart and take the next obvious step.

Ignoring the Value of Awakening

In Buddhism, ignorance is the fundamental cause of delusion, suffering, and transmigration from one life to another. We can maintain ignorance by refusing to acknowledge the eternal source we have touched or by favoring it over human form and experience. The keys to ending suffering are to accept the realization of our true nature and to bring our unique expression into the world.

Facing Conditioning

Some spiritual teachers see previous life memories as ways of recognizing conditioned traits that must be faced to be released. Others say that by recognizing there is no personal self, and knowing yourself to be consciousness, all residual conditioning dissolves. In other words, you must believe in "me" for it to continue. Fundamentally, when an old pattern of conditioning arises, we need to meet it with honesty and self-reflection.

It can come as a surprise that awakening is the beginning, not the end, of transformation. It is extremely rare for a moment of realization to become permanent. But like a sixth sense, knowing never really goes away. Identity falls away and then resurges, yet a sense of radiant presence remains when we attend to it. Changes in our view of who and what we are can be disorienting. This disorientation happens because of human tendencies to create meaning, want familiarity, and seek understanding. They are powerfully programmed patterns of mind, which is why gradual alignment with the truth we have glimpsed is important. We realize that any experience that comes and goes is limited, impermanent, and not the whole of who we are. Awakened consciousness doesn't buy into drifting thoughts or stories about the past or future. We must slowly learn to navigate the world in a new way.

9. Living the Paradox of Duality and Non-Duality

T hose of us raised with Judeo-Christian views of spirituality are generally taught as children to personify God as a powerful being who is watching us from a distance and determining our fates. This perception is embedded at such an early age, before reasoning develops, that it permeates our emotional relationship with the sacred. We might see ourselves as sinful, guilty, lower than, and obedient to a force who knows better than we do. We pray for favors or special dispensations to something "other." If tragedy strikes and we lose a loved one or suffer a difficult trauma, we can end up blaming God and severing our relationship with sacredness entirely.

When I began exploring the dynamics of awakening, I struggled to understand what the Christian mystics were describing because I had been raised in a church with a hierarchical structure that depends on duality and a theological bias that separates humans from God. Generally, Christians are encouraged to trust and to worship, to believe and to obey, but never to strive to become God. I once imagined Christian saints to be people who saw visions of Jesus or of divine light, who received direct messages from this distant God. After careful reading, I came to see that mystics describe moments of union with everything. Jesus can be seen as a non-dual teacher because he made statements such as "I and the Father are one" and "The kingdom of God is within." Many early Christian mystics have offered similar guidance, based on their own experiences of union. Saint Gregory of Nyssa wrote:

> When God made you he imprinted an imitation of the perfection of His own nature upon the structure of our nature, just as one would impress upon wax the outline of an emblem. You must wash away the dirt that has come to

cling to your heart like plaster and then your divine beauty will once again shine forth.[59]

He describes a process of transformation similar to what I have offered in this book. In 1911, Evelyn Underhill described the mystic as one who seeks conscious union with a living, absolute God. She believed Christianity provided the most evolved teachings for mystical union, especially through the doctrine of the Trinity.[60]

The challenges of spiritual awakening that Eastern practitioners report can also be found in the literature of Christian mystics: darkness, emptiness, visions, voices, internal guidance, light, energy, and feeling detached from the body. For Underhill, the experiences of radiance and light were "illumination," a step prior to a full mystic realization. This parallels the yogic descriptions of third-eye chakra experiences when kundalini rises and yogis see the light of a thousand suns prior to full union with the absolute. To me, this suggests that while there are infinite paths of awakening into liberation, we are all awakening to the same reality.

Pathways of Realizing Union with the Absolute

To show how humans have been journeying a variety of paths, from awakening glimpses to liberation, here is a summary of two ways people discover truth in traditions stemming from Vedanta philosophy. In this view of the cosmos, the absolute reality is that all phenomena, every dimension of the universe both known and hidden, emerges from one source. Both schools of thought acknowledge this ultimate principal is free from form or thought or substance.

The first approach to discovering this mystery makes use of our sense of separation, as humans and as form. It views ultimate source as *apparently* separate from humanity and form. This school is based on the ancient *Yoga Sutras of Patanjali*, collected from philosophical and practice traditions that had long been part of Indian culture.

Practitioners use discrimination, devotion, ritual, and yoga practices to gradually release all human attachments in order to know their true self (called *atman*) as an integral part of ultimate reality.

The second way of approaching the absolute proposes there is only one existence, inclusive of all. All form is only a manifestation of the one. In the West this concept is known as non-duality. *Advaita-Vedanta*—which means "the non-dual end of the Vedas"—is a teaching that comes from the *Upanishads,* and is a basis of the puranic and tantric literature. Traditional practitioners use study, meditation, and transmission as transforming portals, and follow a gradual path to return, step-by-step, to the source of manifestation. A core principal is that the transcendental core of our being is identical with the transcendental core of the universe itself (known as *Brahman*) and that we are reincarnated until we become liberated.[61] Many modern non-dual teachers in the West emphasize sudden awakening over gradual practices that are more concerned with the physical and energetic body systems. In some cases, they believe simply hearing the truth can be enough to trigger realization.

The Duality of Spiritual Practice

Doing practices to foster spiritual development is inherently dualistic because it suggests we are separate from our source or from God. Most practices evolved from traditions that support gradual clearing and purifying to return to a direct experience of our true nature or transcendent source. They tend to encourage devotion and chanting to open the heart, and intense dancing or sacred rituals to evoke the sacred.

Our mind functions in a world of division: continually creating subjects and objects, making comparisons between one stage and another, categorizing concepts and behaviors. As a result, most spiritual systems are built on a platform of duality that our mind can accept. Teachers continue to develop innovative systems to support a broad spectrum of followers. Many processes have evolved to make the most of particular frameworks and styles of teaching, such as physicality, concentration, resonance with sound, devotion, intellectual study, silent sitting, movement, dance, and imagining deities and shapes. Since humans have diverse styles of learning, each approach to spiritual awakening is attractive to certain people. Each will serve as a portal for someone, but none will work for everyone.

The Non-Duality of Going Beyond

The view of non-duality takes a spiritual seeker beyond the mind, beyond a belief system, and ultimately beyond a personal self as a character and an identity. This going beyond is not the end of thought, but the end of addiction to the messages thoughts offer. It makes periods of inner silence possible. It is freedom from being tied to personal conditioning and the chattering mind. Often we become open to non-dual view only after we have had enough exposure to spiritual practices to realize this: no matter how many mystical moments we have, or how much our worldview has changed, there is still a sense that something is missing. The urge to seek a permanently transcendent state is itself a dualistic thought. It is based on something impossible, because all experiences pass. And the "me" who longs for them is an illusion. Realizing this gives way to the question, "Is this all there is?"

When I look out the window, if I am not wearing my glasses, everything looks misshapen. Then I put on my glasses. Things take their natural size and shape, and I realize how distorted my perception can be. The shift in how awareness perceives the world through dual and non-dual perspectives is very similar.

Dreams offer a wonderful example of how we appear separate, while being united in one vast consciousness. We can experience imaginal forms in dreams that seem separate from us, even though they arise within us during sleep. Sometimes we feel our self at the center of the dream experience, where events happen to a "me." Other times we seem to be a watcher, an observer as the dream unfolds. As awareness, we witness apparently "other" individuals and apply labels and stories to them, causing us to feel separation. However, these others are our own consciousness taking a variety of forms. In the same way, in waking reality universal consciousness projects many collective images—all its forms—so together we can call this a "world" and navigate it as a group, family, culture, and species.

Many spiritual teachers describe liberation as being like turning off the film projector of life's movie. When we release all the varied projections of our mind, consciousness remembers itself. Not distracted by characters and plotlines, consciousness recalls its essence as a vast expanse of stillness. Consciousness perceives its own depth and breadth, without boundary, which holds the potential for unlimited projection as forms. The separate self is seen as illusory—just one of these forms. Consciousness awakens out of the dream of separation when our body-mind is ready to abandon its projected positions, concepts, and attachments in order to be the truth of unity.

Non-dual view shifts perception about the nature of reality. In moments when our sense of presence arises, when we feel ourselves to be open and awake to absolute consciousness, we are unencumbered by thought and judgment. Suddenly the world's problems appear to be caused by human blindness to our true nature and ignorance of our connectedness to one another. None of us is to blame because no one really exists in the way we believe.

The Illusory View of Personal Duality

The shared illusion that we are only physical forms driven by thoughts, opinions, and emotions keeps us confused about the nature of reality and our natural role within it. This illusion locks each of us into conditioned thought and behavior until that is shattered by the explosive recognition of awakening.

Human thought produces reasons for us to doubt, blame, rage, attack, hide, and fear. These emotions are universal and we often project them onto others as well as ourselves. From an awakened perspective, it is as painful to watch a person hate and reduce herself or himself as it is to watch her or him hate and reduce another. It is painful because we see how these patterns and beliefs are deluded, false, and destructive.

Every spirit, or presence, enters the world as a spark of potential and a package of talents that is open to love and be loved. If this birthright is lost, it is usually because of distorted perception caused by rejection, grief, trauma, neglect, verbal or physical abuse, and other injury. When love is not encouraged and nourished, it recedes deep into the heart and we armor our self against soft feelings, often at an early age. Our genuine human need for recognition and connection is warped.

The distortion can be severe, as a belief arises that "I am bad," or "Others are bad," or "All humans are bad and my genuine expression in life is unsafe." As a result, we can see streaks of hatred, rage, and prejudice in people who wield power in the world. And we can see people turn the same qualities inward, against themselves, because they feel powerless and believe their lives do not matter. Both are blind to the power and beauty of our true nature, and the possibility of enjoying the expression of human potential.

Putting on the Non-Dual Lens

Non-dual perception can return us to our natural state of openness and appreciation. It does not devalue human experience; it enhances our ability to see innate possibilities we have suppressed. This vision is all-inclusive, holding the vastness of many realms of existence, the core of emptiness, and the dynamic creativity of everyone's unique human experience.

Humanness—and all the other forms in nature, alive or not— cannot be isolated from oneness. We are all the ways that emptiness dances into form, which is best described in the poetic and insightful Buddhist *Heart Sutra*. A non-dual view sees existence as appearances radiating in energetic vibrations from one vast stillness, or potential. God is all-encompassing, the one consciousness in multitudes of forms. Some non-dual teachers point students toward the realization of being "nothing": no thing, emptiness. Paradoxically, they teach that realization reveals we are everything, the endless universal self. This is pointing to a realization that is beyond language, that cannot be contained in words. When we experience nothingness, our mind stops superimposing ideas of what liberation is. There is nothing to grasp or hold on to. We become stillness.

Non-duality is a way of experiencing life beyond any belief we may have about it. It points toward liberating attachment to a separate "me" and this brings psychological freedom and peace. When consciousness gives up duality as a way of looking at the world, it feels alive by simply *being*, as opposed to being caught in the complexity of divisive thinking. We intuitively recognize that underneath all appearances there is one spacious consciousness, which contains all, and that each of us at the core is this spacious consciousness.

Upon reflection, most of us can understand the interconnectedness of all things. We can see that without air, water, sun, trees, and the gifts of nature, we could not exist as a species. We can see that humanity shares the same needs, that we are part of nature. Our bodies are natural expressions of life and our uniqueness is how nature's variations unfold, with our unique heritage, conditioning, energetic style, intelligence, inclinations, and talents. It is natural for us to identify with this, but when consciousness awakens we see that separateness and uniqueness are ways of identifying with the body and conditioning that limits our understanding.

Thinking in Non-Duality

Awakening is a direct, intuitive remembrance of ourselves as the essence of life. Before all the experiences and conditioning were attached and our thoughts became the apparent managers of our life, there was non-duality. As soon as thinking takes over all is divided, all appears to be dual: birth and death, awake and asleep, myself and other, light and dark, like and dislike, good and evil. These are the perceptions of our separate self that seem to help us navigate the world. To be enlightened is to be undivided, while living with the paradox of division. It is mysteriously both emptiness and interdependence, stillness and flow.

The mind cannot understand non-division. It assumes that gathering and organizing facts, memories, and experiences is essential. And to some degree this is true: the rules for the world of form require us to understand certain relative facts like "I cannot physically fly off a building," "I cannot ingest poison if I want to stay embodied," "I can learn to drive and operate machinery," "I can set up time in days, months, and years." These are activities of the "working" aspect of mind. They are rules for the relative world.

Some non-dual teachers appear to say that thought must stop or will stop if we become enlightened, and this is not something to fear. We do not become helpless and limited, as that would just waste our potential. These teachings point beyond limitations of thought. We need to be willing to live in the vastness of open space and trust that we will survive. To awaken, we need to reach deeper than thoughts, into an openness that is empty of thought. This is the pure awareness that exists before thought-forms arise.

In no-mind or empty-mind, we perceive beyond mind. While in no-thought, we can perceive truth. Some have called enlightenment "the dissolution of mind," but it is closer to a transparency, an inner space free of the illusory, transient, conditioned, and often irrational nature of thought. Thoughts may arise but they do not stick. As we recognize how we have been attached to our self as a unique but transient character, we take our self and others less seriously, we become less compulsive and ego-driven. The illusory ego gains power by believing thoughts and attaching to them, so it gradually falls away when truth is seen and lived. When thoughts and even feelings are perceived to be energies moving through a system rather than "who I am," we cannot sustain belief in a separate self.

An irony in this process is that, however we go forward, we end up in the same place. It is the place where we began as spirit, as awareness entering the experience of humanity. We are *being* responding to *what is*. After realization, we return to this ordinary life because we are not truly free until we can live openly and spaciously, free from resistance to the life in the world that we have created. This is sometimes called "embodiment," which I'll discuss more in the next chapter.

This is the path to feeling at peace with life and death, to ending the inner turmoil that comes with division, and to completing the search for what matters: what is real in a transient life. When we clearly see the separate self as simply a dance of energies in a creative movement of nature, and we allow what we experience to flow through without struggle, our life becomes freer and more immediate. The present moment brings more joy than planning for the future or dwelling on the past. We feel simple, intimate, and relaxed.

Avoiding the Extremes

If we relate with non-duality as yet another string of beliefs, it becomes just as sticky, liable to trap us in mind and mislead us. Beliefs cannot end our seeking any more than a picture of ice cream can satisfy our craving for it.

When consciousness shifts, we can initially perceive that nothing exists, that forms are appearances only. With this view, all is regarded as an illusory dance in vastness and there is nothing to be concerned about. We can feel reassured at first, but if our mind takes hold of this idea and begins to assume this is all there is, so nothing matters, we may fall into depression, despair, passivity, and nihilism. This happens because this view is an interpretation of mind rather than an understanding of how things are, and dwelling in it is a great loss. If we indulge this tendency of mind, we might get stuck in it for a long time. It can become an endlessly long winter, when all seems dead. But we can also remember that "nothing matters" means we are free to move in new directions and give up inhibitions. We can abandon our self-consciousness, as Laurie discovered.

Laurie was very shy about public speaking. She had this experience of what can arise from nothing, which was so profound that she went on to become an internationally renowned speaker in her field of expertise.

> I was meditating alone late at night when my mind seemed to slip out of my body, and my consciousness drifted in a space that was like the Milky Way. I felt merged into a vast, etheric, light and love. When I came out of this trance-like state, I was lying on the floor and several hours had passed. My body was vibrating and I felt I was glowing. The next day, all anxiety I had about teaching was gone, and it was clear that I only needed to think that someone in the room might need to hear what I had to say. Then I could be comfortable speaking in front of a group.

In the other extreme, awakening may reveal that from the nothingness of ether and boundless space, everything arises. One infinite consciousness is exploding in myriad forms and dances. We can experience heightened perception, in which the smallest flower expresses glory and love. Life can happen in a natural flow, seemingly providing all that is needed in each moment. There can be spontaneous and irrational compassion and joy, even in the most trying circumstances. This eternalism can be so blissful and full that we think this is the only way to be so we resist anything unpleasant.

We need to go inward to question and discover our realization of truth, beyond thoughts, beliefs, assumptions, and feelings. As Adyashanti said about his liberation,

> What I saw…was that I am everything and I am nothing, and also I am beyond everything and nothing. I saw that what I am is inexpressible. It had the sense of going through and through and through—right to the very root of existence."[62]

In the stillness between extremes, we'll discover who we are. Possibilities will arise from the heart and the deeper intuition of the gut so a new birthing can happen. Our natural impulse toward life as an expression of love, wisdom, and creativity can emerge without barriers.

Whether you have seen that you are *nothing* or you are *everything*, there is a need in the human form to live, to move, and to express. We may perceive our self to be a real, separate being, or we may view everything as simply a dream. Regardless, we are a participant in the flow of humanity. Even if we realize we have no control, we have a role that no one else can perform. We each make our unique mark on the world because all of us are part of the expression of the one. Each facet of this universal jewel is relevant. We are the aspects of God that move the consciousness of the planet forward. Whatever happens to you is happening to God. Whatever your response, it is God's response.

When you pull all that psychic energy out of the ego's project of maintaining a separate self, where will you put it? Your energy was wrapped up in illusion. As it becomes freer, return again and again to the lens that corrects perception. Let your energy be infused with truth and love, and become a positive force. This is the invitation to an embodied, awakened spirit. You may as well embrace it and live it out, all the way. Your life is what spirit gets to enjoy through you.

10. Embodied Gift of Being

L iberation is a time of returning to the world with awareness of who we truly are, without resistance to life, form, or engagement. While we may feel an urge to escape the world, we are not attached to it because in liberation we discover our essential contribution to the whole. We are open to being spontaneously guided by the universe, as it needs us. We respect humanness and the sacredness of all life, even with its illusory existence, as we perceive the oneness underneath the apparent diversity. As liberated beings, we are undivided because we have released demands on, and resistances to, what is. If an emotion erupts occasionally, we have no resistance; we turn to face it and discover its roots with curiosity. We find freedom in not needing to inflict our inner eruption on others, and it passes like a strong gust of wind.

Liberation Is an Embodied Return

Awakening is both a sudden shift (a quantum leap in perspective and sense of *who I am*) and gradual shift (as the rest of our psyche and body-mind catches up to support change). What can take the longest time is liberation. Realization frees us from constraining belief systems and emotional patterns, but true liberation is demonstrated in how we live the realization, something commonly referred to as embodiment. This use of the word is different from chapter 7, where it describes ways to energetically inhabit our body with awareness. Here, embodiment is the lived expression of our true nature.

When we are awakened, the entire world is one divine dance, arising from nothing, ever fresh and new, and it seems as if our old life was a dream. It can be like arriving suddenly on another planet and, knowing nothing of the territory, we need a lengthy period of orientation. Zen Buddhists call this being a "baby Buddha," and some say it can take as long as twelve years. We slowly unfold into a liberated life.

As realization becomes embodied, we participate in the world as part of a natural flow of things with a sense of calling. A few may stay in caves or monasteries, but the modern pull is to return and be of service. This is not an injunction or a mental attitude, it is an urge of the heart. We sense that, if we need to escape from the world in order to be free, we are not so free after all. When we can only feel happy abiding in the emptiness of pure consciousness, we are just as stuck as if addicted to worldly attachments. Both activity and passivity, giving and receiving, participating and meditating, are part of how we move as a whole. So these are the two final steps to liberation: orientation and return.

Of course, nothing is ever final when we live on the edge of the infinite. There is instead a continual recycling of our patterns and gifts in a dance with phenomena. The journey can be drawn as a spiral: consciousness leaps, then returns to collect more of itself as fuel for awakening, then leaps again further into the freedom of realization. After liberation, there is no drive to collect experiences or to go anywhere beyond where we are. There is an ordinariness that comes with a return into life.

I was once told a great metaphor for being awake: it is like being a breeze. I love this metaphor because it reflects the freedom of moving through life without a fixed position, with fluidity, and with full acceptance of everything we touch. It is like love, caressing all existence without stopping to analyze it. It is not separation, nor is it identification. It is the movement of presence with what is.

As humans, there are many things our mind resists and many events that cause pain, suffering, disappointment, and rage. We need to be compassionate with our humanness. We are a process that we are not in control of, and never will be. When we relax into this, we may begin to experience life as a breeze. Embodiment is this kind of relaxation. It allows us to feel oneness and wonder with the many human experiences that arise. Here are the ways teachers describe it from within three different traditions.

The great teacher, Jiddu Krishnamurti, who navigated an extensive spiritual emergence that lasted many years, wrote about an ecstasy that never left him. "I am full of something tremendous. I can't tell you in words what is like a bubbling joy, a living silence, an intense awareness like a living flame."[63]

Father Thomas Keating writes that "the presence of God should become a kind of fourth dimension to all of life. Our three-dimensional world is not the real world because the most important dimension is missing: namely that from which everything that exists is emerging and returning in each micro-cosmic moment of time... The contemplative state is established when contemplative prayer moves from being an experience or series of experiences to an abiding state of consciousness. The contemplative state enables one to rest and act at the same time because one is rooted in the source of both rest and action."[64]

One of the greatest masters of non-duality, the Advaita sage Ramana Maharshi, said that abiding in the cosmic self alone can release us from bondage. But discriminating what is ultimately real from what is unreal "can lead to a distaste for the transient." Then he added, "The profound *jnani* ["devotee of knowledge"] is always rooted in the [cosmic] self alone. He does not think of the universe as 'unreal' nor does he see it as apart from himself."[65]

Until the mind is released from bondage, its tendency is to be self-serving, even capable of ignoring the suffering of others. This makes separation, competition, and anxiety flourish. Awakening washes away these divisions and liberation opens our heart in ways that move us to act so that we are contributing to the whole. This brings compassion, service, and creativity as positive forces for change in the world.

While enlightenment may be described as deep peace and the realization of the truth behind all appearances, this is not to suggest it requires a lifestyle that withdraws from the world into nonparticipation. Instead the longing to know truth, once resolved in liberation, becomes a longing to serve. We long for our unique gifts to be of value to others, to benefit others.

This urge is not a mental inflation: this is not saving the world or attracting multitudes as disciples. There have been great spiritual guides on the planet and yet the world is not yet saved. Only an innocent, inflated, or mentally ill mind would take on such a task.

This urge to serve does not come from the shadowy vibrations of anger, resistance, or right-and-wrong thinking that fuel many people to push for change in the world. Such forces move slowly because their aggression produces resistance and pushback. When social change is fueled by recognition of oneness, there is no separation, so along with positive vision, love, and compassion, a spark of new potential is lit that everyone can explore together. This empowers true benefit. As Adyashanti has pointed out "To give up being either ignorant or enlightened is the mark of liberation and allows you to treat others as your self. What I am describing is the birth of true love."[66]

Service is often a one-on-one task, beginning with oneself, and following a quiet impulse to do what can be done with the understanding we have been given. By seeing clearly that everything is as it is, and releasing the resistance to life as it is, we become more capable of moving into what *can* be, and transmitting this possibility to others as they become available to hear it. We also begin to listen without judgment to others' needs.

Gradually, collectively, new potentials arise in our world of form that are made of opposites, and can be dark and distressful or light and inspiring. We embrace all because ultimately our liberation is not personal but exists for the interactions that serve the whole. It can serve the evolution of our greater collective mind, as the mystics Sri Aurobindo and Teilhard de Chardin believed. Liberation is not perfection in a human body. Nor does it make life perfect and without challenges. Instead it pulls life into a flow, with imperfections, that we accept. This ability to meet whatever arises along the way with acceptance brings equanimity.

Fogginess of mind gives way to more clarity as we perceive things ever closer to how they are. The barriers in the heart dissolve, which leads us to perceive boundaries between "me" and others as illusory.

Even the boundaries between life and death dissolve. We appreciate the miracle of existence happening, in all its glory, as well as the miracle of being able to be a human being. These are precious gifts, however temporary or challenging.

Enlightenment is returning home to where we have always lived, but never recognized until we moved into, and through, the journey of awakening. The spirit that leapt forward offered itself from the depths to be discovered, known, and lived.

ACKNOWLEDGMENTS

I am touched by the heartfelt openness of the many people who shared their stories and challenges with me over the years, and grateful beyond measure for all they have taught me. Each one has contributed so much to my understanding of the amazing processes that accompany spiritual awakening and realization. Because of their generosity, readers may find fresh perspectives, understanding, and support for awakening.

Many remarkable teachers, therapists, and friends were instrumental to my personal journey by offering suggestions, practices, healing, insight, wisdom, inspiration, encouragement, and transmission. I am incredibly graced by those who have crossed my path. I am especially grateful to: Adyashanti and Mukti for their demonstrations of love and truth in our world; my early colleagues in the Kundalini Research Network who provided a foundation for my work; the faculty who supported my research at the Institute of Transpersonal Psychology; the yogis who have offered me historical perspectives; the pioneering work of Stanislov and Christina Grof who founded the Spiritual Emergence Network; my travel guides and companions in India and Switzerland; my friends and students at Shanti River Center; and my patient husband, Bill, who provided a supportive foundation for many adventures.

I am blessed by those at Non-Duality Press and New Harbinger Publications who provided this opportunity to share what I have learned, believing readers will benefit from it, and by my editor, Jennifer Holder, for her wisdom and help to shape and create this book.

We are all companions, mysteriously connected as oneness. We assist each another—sometimes without knowing all the ways we were an influence—in this collective awakening to our true nature. Every life that has touched mine is now touching yours. And you, in turn, will be a light for others.

RESOURCES

This is a partial list of resources that are helpful in a spiritual awakening process. For a more extensive list, please visit the annotated booklists pages at http://www.kundaliniguide.com/ and http://www.awakening guide.com/.

Websites for Referrals

The European Transpersonal Association: http://eurotas.org/

International Spiritual Emergence Network: http://www.spiritual emergencenetwork.org/

Australian Spiritual Emergence Network: https://www.spiritual emergence.org.au/

United Kingdom Spiritual Crisis Network: http://spiritualcrisis network.uk/

Conferences, Interviews, and Non-Dual Teachings

Bonnie Greenwell: My website with articles about the awakening process and contact information is http://www.awakeningguide .com/. The website that offers an overview of the kundalini process is http://www.kundaliniguide.com/. My *Awakened Living* blog is found at https://shantiriver.wordpress.com/.

Adyashanti: A very clear and inspiring non-dual teacher who offers many downloads of writings, talks, and videos related to spiritual awakening at http://www.adyashanti.org/.

The Association of Transpersonal Psychology: An international coordinating organization of people dedicated to scientific, social, and clinical transpersonal work offers information and a directory at http://www.atpweb.org/.

Buddha at the Gas Pump: An Internet and YouTube program of weekly interviews with a broad selection of more than 400 spiritual teachers and "ordinary" spiritually awakened people that you can find at https://batgap.com/.

International Society for the Study of Subtle Energies and Energy Medicine (ISSSEEM): A forum that holds annual conferences at Unity Village in Missouri and produces a journal focused on integrative healing, subtle energy, and energy medicine. More information is at http://issseem.org/.

Institute of Noetic Sciences: A nonprofit organization dedicated to research into the individual and collective transformation of consciousness. Hosts events in the US and Europe. You can learn more at http://noetic.org/.

Science & Nonduality: An organization of scientists and non-dual teachers that holds annual conferences in the US and Italy. More information is at https://www.scienceandnonduality.com/.

Books for Further Study

Adyashanti, *The End of Your World* (Boulder, CO: Sounds True, 2008) describes many of the changes and challenges that occur after an initial awakening of consciousness.

Adyashanti, *Falling into Grace* (Boulder, CO: Sounds True, 2010) is a great introduction to awakening for those who are beginning a spiritual search.

Cornell, Judith, *Mandala: Luminous Symbols for Healing* (Wheaton, IL: Quest Books, 2006) offers guidelines and many examples for using mandala art to connect to the sacred within.

Greenwell, Bonnie, *The Kundalini Guide* (Ashland, OR: Shakti River Press, 2014) is a guidebook to navigating the kundalini process.

Greenwell, Bonnie, *The Awakening Guide* (Ashland, OR: Shakti River Press, 2014) is a guidebook exploring the phenomena that arise after spiritual awakening.

Harrigan, Joan Shivarpita, *Kundalini Vidya: A Comprehensive System for Understanding and Guiding Spiritual Development* (Knoxville, TN: Patanjali Yoga Care, 2000) offers a classical kundalini model in detail, as taught by a tantric tradition in India.

Judith, Anodea, *Eastern Body, Western Mind: Psychology and the Chakra System as a Path to the Self* (Berkeley: Celestial Arts, 2004) shares a comprehensive overview of the chakra system with detailed descriptions of each one that show they represent the way we are organized to cope in our lives.

Stayananda, Swami Saraswati, *Kundalini Tantra* (Bihar, India: Bihar School of Yoga, 1984) gives an excellent overview of the kundalini tradition and philosophy, including experiences and practices to awaken and nurture the process.

Singh, Kathleen, *The Grace in Dying: A Message of Hope, Comfort and Spiritual Transformation* (San Francisco: HarperOne, 2000) was written by a Buddhist hospice psychologist to describe how people can enter awakening during the dying process.

Tirtha, Swami Visnu, *Devatma Shakti: Divine Energy* (Rishikesh, India: Yoga Shri Peeth Trust, 1980) is a classical Indian book by a respected authority who describes the subtle-body system and experiences that accompany a kundalini awakening.

Various Authors, *Kundalini Rising: Exploring the Energy of Awakening* (Boulder, CO: Sounds True, 2009) collects twenty-six essays by teachers, scholars, and researchers that describe their perspectives on kundalini awakening.

NOTES

1. Adyashanti, *Emptiness Dancing* (Los Gatos, CA: Open Gate Publishing, 2004) 77.

2. Sharon Landrith, in conversation, March 2017.

3. Eckhart Tolle, *The Power of Now* (Novato, CA: New World Library) 1, 2.

4. For more on the masts, see http://www.meherbabadnyana.net /life_eternal/Book_One/Masts.htm.

5. Swami Visnu Tirtha, *Devatma Shakti: Divine Energy* (Rishikesh, India: Yoga Shri Peeth Trust, 1980) xix.

6. Daniel C. Matt, *The Essential Kabbalah* (San Francisco: HarperCollins, 1996) 106.

7. Joan Shivarpita Harrigan, *Kundalini Vidya: The Science of Spiritual Transformation* (Knoxville, TN: Patanjali Yoga Care, 2000) 103–20.

8. Swami Ambikananda Saraswati, *Healing Yoga* (New York: Da Capo Press, 2001) 304.

9. Harrigan, *Kundalini Vidya*. This book offers a unique description of the nadis. The author is a psychologist and yogi who spent many years with Swami Chandrasekharanand. He initiated her in his kundalini yoga lineage and taught her its detailed kundalini science. It is more complex and complete than any system I have come across. I recommend her book, especially if you are drawn to a dedicated yogic lifestyle. Her website is http://kundalinicare.com/.

10 Saraswati, *Healing Yoga*, 102–75.

11. George Feuerstein, *Tantra: The Path of Ecstasy* (Boston: Shambala Publications, 1998) 229–49.

12. Saraswati, *Healing Yoga*, 174–5.

13. Swami Sivananda, "Illustrations in Vedanta," *The Divine Life Society website*, accessed October 20, 2017, http://sivanandaon line.org/public_html/?cmd=displaysection&section_id=781.

14. Lao Tzu, *Tao Te Ching*, trans. Jane English and Gia-Fu Feng (New York: Vintage, 1997).

15. Thomas Cleary, *The Secret of the Golden Flower* (New York: Harper, 1991) 55.

16. Andrew Newberg, MD and Mark Robert Waldman, *How Enlightenment Changes the Brain* (New York: Penguin Random House, 2016) 86.

17. Thomas Keating, *Open Mind, Open Heart* (New York: Continuum, 1992) 96.

18. A great version of Saint John of the Cross's text *Dark Night of the Soul* can be found at http://www.carmelitemonks.org /Vocation/DarkNight-StJohnoftheCross.pdf.

19. Matt, *The Essential Kabbalah*, 124.

20. Evelyn Underhill, *Mysticism* (New York: Dutton and Co., 1961) 463–4.

21. Ibid, 304.

22. Andrew Newberg and Daniel Siegel, *Neuroscience Training Summit 2016*, Denver, Colorado, May 10, 2016.

23. National Institute of Complementary and Integrative Health, "Use of Complementary Health Approaches in the U.S." *Most used Mind and Body Practices*, https://.nccih.nih.gov/research statistics/NHIS/2012/mind-body.

24. Yoga Journal and Yoga Alliance, *2016 Yoga in America Study*, https://www.yogaalliance.org/Portals/0/2016%20Yoga%20 in%20America%20Study%20RESULTS.pdf.

25. Ajit Mookerjee, *Kundalini: The Arousal of the Inner Energy* (New York: Destiny Books, 1981) 39.

26. Stayananda, Swami Saraswati, *Kundalini Tantra* (Bihar, India: Bihar School of Yoga, 1984) 14, 101–4.

27. Yang Jwing-Ming, *The Root of Chinese Qigong* (Wolfeboro, NH: YMAA Publication Center, 1997) 6, 280.

28. Cleary, *The Secret of the Golden Flower*, 11.

29. Ibid, 77.

30. JJ Semple, *The Backward-Flowing Method* (Bayside, CA: Life Force Books, 2009). The practices offered by Semple draw on an earlier edition of *The Secret of the Golden Flower*, translated by Richard Wilhelm in 1931.

31. Pancham Singh, trans., *The Hatha Yoga Pradipika* (Delhi: Nataraj Books, 2014) i.

32. Srisa Chandra Vasu, trans., *The Gheranda Samhita* (Delhi: Sri Satguru, 1914) 37–41.

33. Tirtha, *Devatma Shakti: Divine Energy*, 43.

34. The Exploring Psychedelics Conference, June 4–5, 2016, Ashland, OR.

35. Oliver Sacks, *Hallucinations* (New York: Vintage, 2013).

36. Stephanie Marohn, featuring Malidoma Patrice Somé, "The Shamanic View of Mental Illness," *The Natural Medicine Guide to Schizophrenia* (Hampton Roads Publishing, Newburyport, MA, 2003) 178–89.

37. Kathleen Singh, *The Grace in Dying* (San Francisco: HarperOne, 2000) 265.

38. Psychologist Richard Miller developed iRest Yoga Nidra. For more information, see https://www.irest.us/.

39. Sacks, *Hallucinations*.

40. Jana Dixon, *Biology of Kundalini* (Morrisville, NC: Lulu.com, 2008).

41. NHLBI (National Heart, Lung, and Blood Institute). National Sleep Disorders Research Plan, 2003. Bethesda, MD: National Institutes of Health; 2003.

42. Sacks, *Hallucinations*.

43. Jana Dixon's website, http://www.biologyofkundalini.com, offers a long list of supplements she recommends for various kundalini issues.

44. Many find that the Gayatri Mantra effectively awakens sacred wisdom and intelligence. A translation and discussion of its meaning can be found in Sadguru Sant Keshavadas' book *Gayatri: The Highest Meditation* (Delhi: Motilal Banarsidass, 1978).

45. Christina Grof and Stanislav Grof, *The Stormy Search for the Self* (New York: Tarcher, 1992).

46. B. S. Goel, *Third Eye and Kundalini* (Bajagaan, India: Third Eye Foundation of India, 1995) 10–11.

47. D. Lukoff, F. Lu, and R. Turner, "Toward a More Culturally Sensitive DSM-IV: Psychoreligious and Psychospiritual Problems," *The Journal of Nervous and Mental Disease* 180, no. 11 (Nov 1992).

48. In 2016, the Grofs founded the International Spiritual Emergence Network as a referral network for people in a spiritual crisis: http://www.spiritualemergencenetwork.org/.

49. Goel, *Third Eye and Kundalini,* 150.

50. The beautiful 1972 movie *Siddhartha* depicts these aspects of the Buddha's story.

51. This practice can be found at http://www.adyashanti.org/.

52. Explore his life and art more through the Nicholas Roerich Museum: http://www.roerich.org/.

53. For an excellent introduction to the meaning and potential of mandala art, see *Mandala: Luminous Symbols for Healing* by Judith Cornell, PhD (Wheaton, IL: Quest Books, 2006). She has also created *The Mandala Healing Kit* (Boulder, CO: Sounds True, 2006).

54. Adyashanti, "The Way of Liberating Insight," online study course, session 7, 2015.

55. Antonio Damasio, "The Quest to Understand Consciousness," TED, March 2011, https://www.ted.com/talks/antonio _damasio_the_quest_to_understand_consciousness.

56. Tom Thompson, "Awakening from the Autobiographical Self," *The Awakened Heart Center*, http://www.theawakenedheart center.com/autobiographical_self.htm.

57. For more on the working mind, see http://noaimiloa.live journal.com/34149.html.

58. For more on this, see Chögyam Trungpa's book *Cutting Through Spiritual Materialism* (Boston: Shambhala Publications, 2002).

59. Gregory of Nyssa, *From Glory to Glory*, ed. Jean Danielou (New York: Scribner's, 1961) 98.

60. Underhill, *Mysticism*, 43.

61. Georg Feuerstein, *Encyclopedic Dictionary of Yoga* (New York: Paragon House, 1990) 10.

62. Adyashanti, *The End of Your World* (Boulder, CO: Sounds True, 2008) 118.

63. Mary Lutyens, *Krishnamurti: The Years of Awakening* (New York: Farrar, Strauss and Giroux, 1974) 282.

64. Thomas Keating, *Open Mind, Open Heart* (New York: Continuum Publishing Company, 1992) 75.

65. *Sri Ramana Maharshi* website, "Importance of Self-Abidance," accessed October 20, 2017, https://sriramanamaharishi.com /ramana-gita/importance-of-self-abidance/.

66. *Adyashanti* website, "How You Treat Others," accessed October 20, 2017, http://www.adyashanti.org/index.php?file=writings _inner&writingid=14.

Bonnie L. Greenwell, PhD, is a transpersonal psychotherapist, author, and non-dual spiritual teacher in Adyashanti's lineage. She has specialized for more than thirty years in mentoring people going through transformative experiences related to spiritual awakening and the kundalini process, which was the subject of her doctoral research at the Institute of Transpersonal Psychology (ITP). Greenwell has an eclectic background, including work in psychiatric units, at a rehabilitation center, as director of the Transpersonal Counseling Center at ITP, and years of private practice. Before finding her ground in non-dual teachings, she studied Jungian psychology; Jin Shin Do® acupressure; Psychotropic and Radiance Breathwork; kundalini, kriya, and Ashtanga yogas; and many Buddhist meditation practices. The founder and former director of the Kundalini Research Network, she has lectured and trained therapists in Europe, Australia, and the United States. Greenwell also established the Shanti River Center for non-dual education and counseling in Ashland, OR.

Foreword writer **Adyashanti** is an American-born spiritual teacher devoted to serving the awakening of all beings. His teachings are an open invitation to stop, inquire, and recognize what is true and liberating at the core of all existence. Adyashanti is author of *The Way of Liberation, Falling into Grace, Emptiness Dancing, True Meditation,* and *The End of Your World.* Based in California, he lives with his wife, Mukti, and teaches throughout North America and Europe, offering satsangs, weekend intensives, silent retreats, and a live Internet radio broadcast.